Praise for Picking Over the Bones

"This is a wonderfully enjoyable read. I think many of us might have driven through Tifton, stopped for lunch, and hurried on, thinking we'd seen the place. Judith Ireland shows us different. Her details are so particular, her nuances so layered, her observations so flavorful, she draws me into experiencing this little '50s town in Georgia as more than just a town, it's a world. For me, as I read these stories, Tifton begins to feel familiar: I feel like I know this place. It reminds me of my own hometown growing up, my own childhood and teenage years—which is curious, because my hometown and childhood were nothing like Ireland's. The emotions are my own but the memories evoking them are hers: it's almost as if I'm "remembering" her life as my own. That's what the best memoirs do: they let us experience what the world would be like if we were someone else; and that's what Judith Ireland achieves in *Picking Over the Bones*."

–Tamim Ansary, author of *West of Kabul, East of New York*

Picking Over the
BONES
a memoir

by JUDITH IRELAND

edited by LANCE ÜMMENHOFER & ERICKA M. ARCADIA
designed by THEO HALL

APRIL GLOAMING

Publisher's Cataloguing-in-Publication Data

Ireland, Judith
Picking over the bones / written by Judith Ireland / designed by Theo
Hall
ISBN: 978-1-953932-16-7

1. Memoir I. Title II. Author

Library of Congress Control Number: 2022949674

This is dedicated to the people in all small towns who understand the African proverb, "It takes a village to raise a child."

This is a work of creative nonfiction. The events and characters are portrayed accurately according to my memory, but it should be noted that memory is not factual. Conversations should not be taken as word for word transcripts although they do represent the feel and spirit of the actual conversations. The dialogue language is consistent with the language of the 1950s, not the language of the modern day in order to facilitate a more accurate account of the times. Most of the names have been changed to protect the privacy of individuals. And, in some cases, I have conflated events, have combined two characters into one, and occasionally have embroidered.

Contents

The Pit Stop

SUMMER 2010

The waitress at the Pit Stop quit taking down our orders and stared at us with her mouth open. She took a deep breath, exhaled slowly, and said, "You don't need all that food." She pointed at my husband with the eraser end of her pencil. "You. You just ordered the barbecue sampler platter, *and* the fried green tomatoes appetizer, *and* a garden salad. And you"—she pointed her accusing eraser at me—"said you wanted the chicken platter, *and* a Caesar salad, *and* fried okra." She sounded like a mother chastising greedy children. "The platters are huge, and they already come with French fries and coleslaw and pickles and rolls, and here you are ordering extra salads and appetizers. You don't *need* a blooming onion on top of all that." She looked back at her check pad shaking her head. After a moment, she seemed to think of an out for us, and asked, "Are some other people coming to join you? Are you ordering for them too?"

"No," Jerry said, sheepish. "It's just the two of us."

We are grown people. In fact, we are old people. We don't feel old. We don't look particularly old. But the numbers say we are plenty old enough to make our own decisions about what to eat.

"Look," I said, "we live in California. We don't get to South Georgia very often, and we really love the barbecue here. The barbecue in California is too sweet. It's like whenever you order barbecue out there, they pour a bottle of maple syrup over it before they bring it to you. When we're here at the Pit Stop, we get carried away and want to try everything because it's so, *so* good."

The waitress's name was Karen, as stitched on her apron. She put her pencil hand on her hip and asked, "What are you doing here from California? Did you drive all that way? I've never been out there myself, but my sister got transferred to San Diego last year. She's in the navy."

Jerry interrupted her. "I don't mean to be rude, but if we could please

1

just get the food, it would be great," he pleaded. "We held off having lunch for a couple of hours until we could get here, and I'm starving." The tantalizing smell of barbecue wafted around us, and our empty bellies growled in complaint.

"Don't worry," Karen said. "You'll get fed. I've been working at the Pit Stop for seven years, and I haven't sent anybody away hungry—yet."

I smiled at her to let her know I was on her side. "No, we didn't drive. We flew into Atlanta last night and drove down from there this morning. We're on our way to Florida, visiting some friends along the way."

"Ninety percent of the people who stop here are on their way to Florida," Karen said, the clear implication being that my explanation was unremarkable.

"But I was born and grew up in Tifton," I said, hoping to differentiate myself from the masses. "When we come through Georgia, we always have lunch here at the Pit Stop, and then we drive into town and look around for a while before we leave, just so I can see it again."

Karen's face softened a little as soon as she heard that I was a member of the tribe. "Oh," she said. "What's your name? Do you still have people in town?"

"My maiden name was Ireland, but all of my family left a long time ago, way, way before you were even born."

Karen looked to be in her early forties, pretty and blonde, beginning to show soft wrinkles around her eyes. Mostly though, what showed her age was how tired she was. "Lots of people leave," she said, a vague sadness in her voice. "I could see myself leaving one day. But I'm like you. I'd never learn to eat Yankee barbecue. Have to come back to the Pit Stop to get a fix now and then, to remember how food's supposed to taste. I can understand that."

She went back to her check pad. "All right. I'll bring you some take-out boxes when I bring your meals. You're going to need them. Promise me you'll take all of the food you don't eat with you when you go, OK?"

After Karen got out of earshot, Jerry said, "That's the first time in my life that I've had to wrestle with a waitperson to convince her to let me spend as much money as I felt like doing in a restaurant."

"She just wanted to let us know what we were getting into. And she probably doesn't like to throw away food," I said.

"It's a different world down here."

"I wouldn't argue against that point. It's for sure a different world from New York."

"Yep," he said. "My people will let you order the whole menu if you'd like. No questions asked. No family history required."

As on our previous visits to the Pit Stop, the food was worth the wait. The barbecue sauce was tangy perfection. The French fries were crispy on the outside, hot and creamy inside, like the okra and the green tomatoes. People can disparage fried food all they want to, but when it's done right, there's nothing like a good French fry for making your mouth happy. Karen was correct about the blooming onion, though. We didn't need it, and it was a bit disappointing, pretty much like onion rings anywhere, although the presentation was interesting. I ate more than I should have. Jerry lasted longer than I did, but he finally gave up too, and we packed the leftovers to take with us, like we'd told Karen we would.

We stepped out of the air-conditioned restaurant carrying Styrofoam boxes of barbecue to a blast of hot, humid air, a reminder that we were in South Georgia at the peak of summer. Uncomfortable as it was, there was a familiarity about it that said to me, "You are home."

We had already planned to dedicate a few hours to a tour around the town after lunch before getting back on the interstate to continue our trip, like we always did when we came through here. Even after moving away fifty years ago, I am still tied to the town in my heart, and on the rare occasions I'm in the area, I need to take it in with my own eyes and be reminded that it was real, that it wasn't an illusion.

When we got back in the car outside the restaurant, Jerry told me, as he had on other trips, that I should keep in mind as we drove around that the residents of the town didn't preserve the place and turn it into a museum the moment I left, and there would probably be a number of changes, even since the last time we'd come through ten years ago. Of course I knew all that. Even so, the changes surprised me every time.

The old part of town, the part where I'd grown up, was a couple of miles from the Pit Stop, which was just off the highway. To get there, we had to make our way past a string of hotels and restaurants, identical copies of which could be seen near any interstate in the country. There was a Hilton, an Econo Lodge, an Applebee's, and on and on. The people going in and coming out of those places looked like people anywhere, wearing the same shorts and flip-flops and summer dresses. The landscaping was like commercial landscaping anywhere with the same newly planted palm trees that hadn't figured out yet that they didn't belong here, and the same impatiens that will grow and look showy anywhere in the country. The license plates on the cars were from anywhere. It was as if Tifton, the one I knew, had disappeared and been replaced with a stamped out version of a generic town, Anywhere, USA.

"What did they do with Tifton?" I said. I had a sinking, *Twilight Zone* feeling in my stomach.

"We'll find it," Jerry said. "They couldn't have moved it too far."

We drove on another mile until the street took a slight bend to the left, and although the buildings were new and didn't fit into my memory, something about the particular curvature of the road felt familiar. "Wait!" I said. "Slow down. I think that's where the Varsity is supposed to be."

"Looks like a parking lot to me."

"It was a drive-up hamburger place," I said. "I've told you about it before. When we were teenagers, we used to go there and park for hours, and look at other kids in their cars looking at us, and listen to the radio and try to be cool."

"How cool were you?" Jerry said.

"Not very, but we thought we were."

"That's what counts."

We drove on a few blocks more to where the street bent again to the left, and we were on Main Street. When we got there, Jerry parked, and we got out of the car to walk the two blocks that had constituted the shopping section of town in my day. A yoga studio now occupied the building that had housed the ladies' clothing store where my mother worked as a saleswoman in the 1950s. A computer repair shop, an antique shop that showed items from my childhood in the window, and a taqueria, also lined the street. But there, right where I'd left it in 1960, was the Tift Theater. It was run-down and seedy-looking, but unmistakably the Tift Theater.

"It shrank," I said. "I don't believe it was this small even the last time we were here. The entryway used to be really wide. There were big movie posters in all these display cases that they've boarded up. I remember the ones for *Salome – Dance of the Seven Veils* and *Creature from*

4

the Black Lagoon that showed barely covered bosoms and scandalized the Baptists. And the ticket window was right here. I used to have to reach way up to give my quarter to the woman. It could not have been this small back then."

"I'd bet money on it being the same size it's always been," Jerry said. "Let's go on and drive by those other places you like to see every time we're here."

We found my grandmother's house, and like the Tift Theater, it had shrunk to half its original size. I rechecked the address to confirm it was the correct house. "But the porch used to be really wide and long, and Mama spent hours out here, rocking and crocheting," I said. "She'd hum and sing 'My Little Mohee' while she rocked. She sang under her breath, thank God. She had an awful singing voice. If she'd sung out loud, she'd have scared the children."

We went from there to drive by what used to be the high school, and the junior high, and the houses where my family had lived. Ghosts leapt out and performed little dramas from my past at every turn.

***

When my cousin Carol and I were little, maybe five or six years old, Carol's goldfish died and provided us with more entertainment than it ever had swimming around and around in its glass bowl. My aunt gave us a mason jar for a coffin, and we planned and executed a beautiful funeral for the fish. Since neither of us had ever been to such a ceremony, we had to improvise from what we had overheard from our grandmother, who loved a good funeral. We filled the bottom of the jar with bits of fabric we pilfered from my aunt's quilt scrap stash to make a suitable bed and laid the fish on top of it. Then we dug a hole in the sandbox for the interment. We picked flowers from my aunt's garden and heaped them on top of the sandy mound and created a cross from glued-together Popsicle sticks and planted it at the head of the grave. I preached and we sang "Jesus Loves Me." Carol even cried. I remember feeling pleasantly wrung out afterward, which helped me understand my grandmother's fondness for these events. But that wasn't the end of it. The day after the funeral, Carol asked, "What do you think Goldy looks like now?" The question led to our disinterring Goldy to examine him. "Still dead!" I announced. Thereafter, we dug up the fish every day for a week until my aunt saw what we were doing and made us quit. It was a fascinating exercise to watch him fade from bright gold to dull yellow to gray, and to marvel at the change from a living, swimming being to inert matter.

There is always something of the same feeling now about driving around Tifton. My cousin and I, and our cohort, laid our growing-up years to rest in 1960 when we finished high school and went off on separate journeys, but every so often, I come back to dig us up and pick over the bones to see what I can learn from them that I missed the first time.

Carol and I, as well as our classmates, were war babies, born during World War II. We were a small group by comparison with the Baby Boomers, that great surge of humanity that came flooding into the world in the twenty years after us. They were born in the United States, into a rising tide of optimism and growing prosperity and hope. We weren't.

We were born into a time when fear hung in the air, when our parents and grandparents saw the real possibility that the way of life they had struggled to achieve coming out of the Great Depression could melt into the hell of a world dominated by a Hitler or a Mussolini. Many of our fathers were away, and when they came home, they wore stiff uniforms that felt rough against our baby skin. And when our fathers left, our mothers cried. By the time I was three years old, I could sing "Now Is the Hour That We Must Say Goodbye," with all of its lyrics, and nobody thought it was strange for such a tragic song to issue forth from baby lips.

We learned early what it meant for a house to have a gold star banner displayed in the window, which showed that a family member had died in the war. When we walked down the street in front of a gold star house, we learned to be quiet and reverential while the adults who held our hands as we walked by whispered about the Conleys whose son had died at Guadalcanal, or the Richardson boy who had been on the Bataan Death March. Nobody tried to hide the facts from us. This was life, and we were part of it, and might as well get used to the truth, better sooner than later.

On the brighter side, we learned that we were all immersed in something overwhelmingly important, the salvation of our nation.

We were southerners, and we knew about lost causes. We knew that a world could be obliterated, and it could happen again, this time with an unimaginably dire result. It was imperative that we win this war. We had to dedicate ourselves to that end.

The general sense of "We're all in this together" prevailed, along with the belief that each of us was noble and high-minded and up to the task. There was a great deal of energy and pride about the assumption of that kind of nobility which was also a part of the times. We were wrapped in it—not only the fear and the sadness, but also the pride, the striving toward goodness. I don't know how the location and the years of our birth defined us apart from those born before and after that war, but in some measure they did.

Family
FALL 1942

"Mama" was my grandmother on my father's side. She was the only "Mama" in our family. She owned the name. My mother was "Mother," but then, she'd have been "Mother" in any case. It suited her. My cousin Carol's mother, my Aunt Ethelle, was "Mom," which suited her too. But only my grandmother was Mama.

Right after I came into the world, Mama stood at the window of the newborn nursery at the Tift County Hospital, in Tifton, Georgia, peered in at me, and pronounced me to be the "ugliest baby she had ever seen."

When Mother told the story about Mama calling me ugly, she always chuckled to take away the sting of it, and maybe the story wasn't even true. She couldn't have heard it with her own ears because she wasn't there. She was down the hall in her birthing bed. She had to have been told by some third party. I don't know who it could have been, but Mama denied all her life that she ever said such a thing.

Whether it was true or not, Mama was geared up to find something wrong with my birth from the get-go anyway, since I was just the second baby in the family born in a hospital instead of in her own home where she, the matriarch, had a front-row seat. My cousin Carol had been the first, a few months earlier, but maybe Mama thought that instance was going to be a one-time thing. Then, when my mother also decided on a hospital birth for her second child, I guess it confirmed that a new precedent had been set with Carol. The drama of the whole affair was always going to be stolen from her from then on. Having to see me through that glass, instead of holding me in her arms moments after I arrived, must have been hard on her. She was a loving woman and certainly didn't wish for anything terrible to happen, in spite of her protestations against hospital births. But there I was, red and screaming and long and stringy, and validating all her warnings about taking this most important ritual into the public market, rather than sheltering it in hallowed space. This was what you got—an ugly baby.

My brother, Mama's first grandchild, had been born in Mama's house, where she put a sharp knife under the birthing bed to "cut the pain," although Mother said the knife did no good that she could tell. And yet, Lowell was noted to be a beautiful baby, so beautiful in fact that he won the Most Beautiful Baby in Tifton contest when he was six months old. Case closed. When my mother told the story, she was quick to tack on at the end of it that I didn't stay ugly. Still, it hurt to hear it over and over. And it hurt that Mother told it like it was some kind of joke, but I always just laughed at it anyway. If something hurt, you didn't let anybody know. It was better to suck it up and pretend you were just fine with whatever it was, especially where Mother was concerned.

Mama wasn't opposed to the Tift County Hospital in general. It was a badge of pride for the town of six thousand souls to have its own hospital so people didn't have to drive all the way to Albany, forty miles away, to get treatment. Mama had a bad heart, and she probably had more than a passing interest in the place, as she knew it would likely figure into her own future. But to bring a baby into the world in such a cold setting as a hospital had to feel wrong to her. It was a big change, and I guess at that time her world was changing faster than she could catch up to it. It was late September, 1942, in South Georgia. The country had been at war for almost ten months. I calculated, after I learned about gestation periods and such things, that I probably owed my existence to the fever pitch my parents were in after my father rushed to join the navy following the bombing of Pearl Harbor.

By the time I was born, three of Mama's sons were in the service on active duty. One of my uncles was in the army, another one was in the air force, and my father, the oldest, was in the navy. The youngest son was too young to enlist, but as soon as he turned eighteen, he joined the navy too. Snapshots of the four of them in uniform standing shoulder to shoulder in Mama and Papa's backyard show them all looking sharp, shoes polished to a high shine, and grinning like going to war was sure to be a play party.

Mama said that she was proud of them and that she had no doubts that they'd all come home in one piece. The main thing she worried about was that one of them would come home with a tattoo. "When Wilton joined the navy, I told him I'd just as soon he came home in a box as with a tattoo," she said. "I didn't mean it, but I wanted him to think

I did." In fact, they all came home in one piece, and without a single tattoo among the four of them, at least not any visible ones.

Other than her words concerning body art, the one bit of advice I ever heard from Mama was to "remember who you are." This was a kind of mantra for her. She didn't expound on it too much. The little that she did say about it was that as long as you act in accordance with who you are in your heart, you'll be OK. There's a lot of worse advice offered up to ones' progeny.

***

Mama wasn't born in Tifton. She came down from North Georgia on the train with her family when she was a young teenager. That was around 1910. "It had been an awful sad time," she said. She told me these things when I was a really little kid and she probably didn't think I could even understand what she was talking about, but I did. Kids always know.

Mama continued, "Not long before we left North Georgia, my stepsister died of influenza, then a bunch of other people died of it too. There was a terrible flu epidemic across the whole world some years later, but there was this smaller one in North Georgia around 1909. Anyway, my daddy up and sold the farm, and we took off for South Georgia on the train." Her daddy had been in the state legislature and had a certain amount of standing in the town where they lived, so it was a big deal for them to just leave like that. "I think he wanted to put all that misery up there behind him," Mama said.

Mama's family hadn't been in Tifton very long before she met Papa. Her friends had set her up with his brother, Wylie, who was "friendly and jolly," but Mama didn't like him. "Mr. Cliff was quiet and kind. He was my pick," she said. She always called him "Mr. Cliff," even after fifty years of marriage.

And just like Mama calling Papa "Mr. Cliff," he always called her "Miss Tennie." Papa was born in Tifton. His parents, like Mama's, had migrated down from the cool, forested hills of North Georgia, to the sandy soil and piney woods of South Central Georgia looking for a better life, but they came twenty years before Mama's. His father drove a mule-drawn wagon all the way, over three hundred miles, with his bride and their little bit of furniture and other household supplies, after they heard about opportunities in the sawmill business in Tift's Town. I guess that what they found in that hot, flat land was better than what they left behind, because they stayed. Papa didn't have a lot to say about his family history, or anything else, to tell the truth, so there's not much I know about it, except that they were in Tifton almost from the beginning of the town.

Tift's Town was founded in 1877 by a carpetbagger, Mr. Henry Harding Tift, whose family had a shipbuilding business in Mystic, Connecticut. That was during Reconstruction after the Civil War, when people in the South were doing anything they could to survive. Sometimes that meant selling things, including land, cheap. Mr. Tift essentially stole sixty-five thousand acres of piney woodland in what is now Tift County with an eye to procuring timber for building ships. He set up a saw mill and a village for his workers, and built a railroad system to haul the lumber out of the mills to Connecticut and other points north. In short order, agricultural opportunities on the cleared land developed, and people started growing cotton and tobacco and other crops that let them scratch out a living. With the farming, in addition to the sawmill work and railroad jobs, the population grew. Tift's Town became Tifton.

My great-grandfather Ireland, Papa's father, was still around and living with Mama and Papa when I was really little. He was ancient. He spent his days on the front porch fully attired, like he was going to church, in dress pants and long-sleeved white shirts and neckties and a hat, even in the summer when it was boiling hot, when wearing a long-sleeved shirt was a gruesome kind of torture. His clothes hung loose on him, with the damp collars of his shirts gaping open around his neck, and he looked like he had shriveled up inside them. He died when I was four years old.

He had lost the last two phalanges of the ring and middle fingers on his right hand in the mills. I liked to sit beside him and hold that hand and fondle the nubs. I tried over and over to get him to describe the accident. His rendition was brief. "Fingers got in the way of the blade, sliced 'em off!" No amount of questioning on my part got him to elaborate. He'd move on to another subject instead of letting me in on the gory details. I was forced to use my imagination. I saw images of blood spurting like a geyser, fingers flying into the air, and much excitement and yelling all around.

The spilt blood that soaked into the sandy Tift County soil seemed to be a baptism, proof that our family belonged here. As a child, I could not conceive of myself apart from Tifton. My family and I were embedded in it, had sprung up out of it, and were so entangled with it that our roots could never be teased apart from it.

***

On my mother's side, the Colleys, the roots in Tifton didn't go as deep. My grandfather, Homer, was born in North Georgia in 1890, the fifth of nine children. His father had been a schoolmaster, and Homer followed in his footsteps. After he completed his education, he secured a position as principal of a one-room school in South Georgia, in a county just north of Tifton where he fell in love with one of his students. They married, and after having two sons and a daughter, his wife died of chronic malaria, leaving my grandfather with the three small children. My mother was only a toddler.

Homer sent the children to be cared for by relatives while he rebuilt his life. For the next several years, my mother, Leola, was juggled between a couple of aunts who were kind but already had housefuls of children. The two older boys were sent to live with their paternal grandmother. Homer remarried a few years later. He and his new wife immediately started creating their own family and Leola and her brothers came back to live with them. By the time Leola was a teenager, her father and stepmother had added five additional children to the family. There were more mouths to feed than her father could manage on his school principal's pay. He took a job as a chemical analyst in Albany, moved the family there, and after a couple of years, he went to work with the Treasury Department as a prohibition officer. The Treasury Department moved the family first to Orlando, Florida, and then to Swainsboro, Georgia, where a bootlegger shot him in the jaw while he and another agent were in the process of raiding a still. After many surgeries and hospitalizations, he continued to have violent headaches, and the government finally decided he was permanently disabled and put him on a pension. That was when he moved the family to Tifton so that one of his older sons could live at home while going to a nearby college. It was 1932.

Although the Colleys were Johnny-come-latelies to Tifton by comparison with the Irelands, I saw evidence that my grandfather Colley intended to stay put there. He died from aftereffects of the gunshot wound when I was a baby, so I don't have direct knowledge about his intentions for permanency. However, grainy photographs of him building a two-story house by hand from concrete blocks that he himself molded in wooden frames seemed to me, as a child, to show a man determined to plant his family firmly in that place.

Our presence in Tifton had been baptized with Ireland blood and sealed with Colley concrete. I had to believe I'd live here and die here with the rest of my family forever and ever, until death did us part. Amen.

Little Kathy Fiscus

SPRING 1949

On the Saturday morning before Easter Sunday when I was six, I stood barefooted on Joanie Wilson's front porch, my nose pressed against the screen door, looking into her living room. I called out for her. The wooden door was open, so I knew somebody was home. With most people, you didn't have to wait outside. You just opened the door and went in, but the Wilsons had different ways. They had only moved to Tifton a year ago when Joanie and I were still five. Mrs. Wilson, a pleasant but stern woman, let me know right off that she didn't like me walking in without them saying I could, so I didn't do it anymore. Instead, I stood outside and yelled. That morning, I had to yell, "Joanie!" a second time through the screen before she came running into the living room from the back of the house in her pajamas.

"That girl ith dead," she said before she even reached the door. She talked funny because she had lost her two top, front teeth the week before, and they hadn't had a chance to grow back in yet. "My daddy thaid tho."

Joanie's daddy had been in the army in the war. We knew which branch of the service everybody's daddy had been in. He was a carpenter who could build and fix anything. My mother admired him a lot. My own daddy didn't know how to fix anything, according to Mother. "He has to have help to hang a picture on the wall," she said. I guess it was true, but I didn't like to hear her say it. As far as I was concerned, my daddy was perfect.

And especially that day, I didn't want to hear Joanie talk about how her daddy said Kathy Fiscus was dead. I knew that's who she meant when she said, "That girl is dead." I didn't have to ask. We had heard about Kathy Fiscus on the radio the night before, like everybody else had. But I acted like I didn't know.

"You want to play in Bruce's house?" I asked her through the screen. Bruce was Joanie's Chow dog who had a purple tongue. Mr. Wilson had

14

built him a nice house from leftover pieces of wood from his work, but Bruce didn't like it. Joanie and I got more use out of it than he did. It was big enough that we could go inside it and sit with our backs against the walls, and it was private so we could tell secrets and do stuff nobody else could see. Mainly, Joanie showed me her hernia when we were in there.

Joanie said yes, so we went out in the backyard and crawled into the doghouse. It smelled doggy inside, like Bruce, even though he didn't spend that much time in there himself. I liked that smell because I loved everything about dogs, and I really loved Bruce. We sat next to each other with our legs stretched out and our feet almost touching the opposite wall. We were quiet for a few moments and I thought Joanie was done with talking about Kathy Fiscus. But then she started up again, and I let her talk while I picked at a sandspur on my foot.

"It was on the radio," she said. "The man said she fell in a well and they can't get her out. It's in California. That's where they make picture shows. They want everybody to pray for her, but my daddy said she's dead already anyway."

"You want to show me your hernia?" I asked.

Joanie pulled her pajama bottoms down around her hips to reveal the odd canvas contraption she wore to keep the hernia pushed into her body. Then she slid the canvas aside so I could see the squishy bit of flesh that popped out like a fat worm low below her belly button on her right side. I'd seen it lots of times, but it was still a breath-stopping mystery and whenever she let me see it, I felt the weight of her mother's words when she had told us that if it got poked, it could break open and Joanie might die, or at least have to go to the hospital or something. After I touched it very gently, Joanie covered it up again. Then she went back to Kathy Fiscus.

"I don't know if she's dead. My daddy just said so." I just stared at her again like I didn't know anything about it.

While I walked home after I left Joanie's, I kept thinking about Kathy Fiscus. I remembered what the announcer on the radio had said last night, and how it had been when we heard about her. The announcer had sounded serious, like the way the preacher at church sounded when he said things that made the grown-ups lean forward and listen hard. "Little Kathy Fiscus of San Marino, California, fell into an abandoned well today while playing with her sister. Attempts to rescue the child so far have been unsuccessful. The family is distraught, and asks for the prayers of the country."

I'd fallen into ditches myself and had climbed out with no more than scrapes and bruises. I always had scrapes and bruises anyway, even without falling into a ditch, and they weren't that bad. Last night, I figured that by the time I got down on my knees beside my bed to pray for her, Little Kathy Fiscus would be out of the well having dinner with her family.

How long has she been down there?" I'd asked Daddy then. He was still wearing his postman uniform from work, which made everything he said sound more important to me.

"She fell into it around three o'clock this afternoon. It's seven now, so about four hours."

"Why can't they just go down in the well and get her out?" I asked.

"Because the hole is too narrow. It's only this big around." He held his hand out in a circle. "It's only fourteen inches in diameter. Do you know what a diameter is?"

"A skinny person can get down there," I said.

"Well, honey, they tried that. It didn't work." He had that same sad tone in his voice that the radio announcer had had.

"I could fit down there."

Daddy shook his head. "We'd never let you do that."

He loosened up the necktie on his collar. We were still waiting for Mother to finish dinner so we could eat. I was hungry.

"Did they put some food in the well for her?" I asked.

"I don't know," my daddy said. "What would you like to eat if you were down in a well?"

I hated seeing my daddy so sad and wanted to make him feel better, so I told him I'd want fried chicken and said that he could tie a string onto a drumstick and lower it into the well for me. We laughed about how funny it would be, like instead of trying to catch a fish with a worm, it would be using a chicken leg to catch a little girl.

"I bet they have her out by the time you wake up in the morning," Daddy said.

When Daddy said the blessing before dinner that night, he included a special prayer for Little Kathy Fiscus and asked Jesus to hold her in the palm of His hands.

The next morning, still bleary-eyed from sleep, I asked my mother, "Did she get out of the well?"

"Not yet," she said. The big console radio in the living room was on, and the announcer was talking in his somber voice about Little Kathy Fiscus.

"People all over the country are praying for the child's swift rescue from the abandoned well. President Truman has sent a message to the Fiscus family expressing his and Mrs. Truman's deep concern and saying that they are in prayer for the child."

My mother turned off the radio. "We're going to the movies tonight. *A Letter to Three Wives*, Linda Darnell and Ann Sothern," she said, as if I knew anything about the movie. My mother loved movies and was always going on about movie stars. She was beautiful herself, like a movie star, with black hair and an olive complexion. I had heard her say that, that she had an olive complexion, although I wasn't sure what it meant except that she was dark, and different from me. I was towheaded blonde, like my daddy. Lowell, my brother, was dark like her. Sometimes I thought he was her child, and I was my daddy's.

"Why haven't they gotten her out?" I asked.

"They're trying," she said. "Come eat your breakfast. Lowell's way ahead of you. He's already had his breakfast, and he's gone across the street to play with Jimmy. Why don't you go up and play with Joanie after you eat."

So I did. That was when Joanie showed me her hernia and said Kathy Fiscus was dead. When I got back home from Joanie's, Mother said she wanted to ask Grandmother Colley something about the new dress she was making me for Easter.

Mother and I walked a block up the street to Grandmother's big white house that my grandfather had built with his own two hands and went around to the back door to go in, the way we always did. Before we even got the screen door shut, Grandmother called out from her sewing room, "Have you heard any more about the little girl in California?"

Grandmother Colley was my mother's stepmother. She got some money from the government on account of her husband dying as a result of his service to the country, but it wasn't enough for her to make ends meet, so she had to take on sewing. She'd been a school teacher in her early life, and I always had a feeling she was kind of embarrassed about sewing for other people, even though she was good at it.

Grandmother was a stout woman and always wore a corset, which presented the weird illusion, right through her dresses, that her ribs ran up and down instead of sideways. I always watched myself carefully around her, as she was quick to tell you what you were doing wrong, and slow to crack a smile. She never raised her hand to me, but I thought a lot of times that she would have liked to.

"She's still down in the well," Mother called back. "Haven't gotten her out yet."

We walked through the back hallway to the sewing room. Grandmother sat at her machine with a tape measure around her neck. She was laying out little pattern pieces on green fabric on the fold-down table attached to the machine.

"They aren't going to," Grandmother said. "Child that small. No telling how deep it is. Probably a dozen children every year fall in a well. Not looking where they're going. I knew a boy fell in a well when I was growing up. Never got him out. Had to abandon the well." It sounded like she was more concerned about the lost well than about the boy. She turned around in her chair then and looked at us. "What kind of help do you need?" The dress was yellow, with flowers that Mother had embroidered across the bodice. She liked making me fancy dresses at Easter to show off her work.

"It just doesn't fit her right across the back, kind of bunches up where it should lie smooth," Mother said.

"OK," Grandmother said and told me to put it on, which I did. Then she pulled at it and pinned it here and there.

"Ow!" I yelled and jumped back when she stuck me with a pin.

"I didn't hurt you!" she said. "Be still, or you'll get stuck again!"

When the session with Grandmother was finally over, Mother folded up the dress and put it in her bag, getting ready to leave. "Keep praying for the little girl, Mother," she said.

"That's not how prayer works," Grandmother snapped. "You don't ask God for what you want. You ask Him that His will be done. If it's God's will that the child get out of the well, she'll get out. If it's not, she won't." She sat back down at her sewing machine and picked up the pattern pieces she had been working on before she stopped to help us.

18

Grandmother had a picture of Jesus on the wall in her sewing room, and I wondered if that meant He listened to her more than He did to people who didn't have His picture on the wall. We didn't have a picture of Jesus in our house.

Grandmother went on talking to my mother as she fiddled with the work on her machine table. "When your daddy was dying, I prayed night and day that he would get better, but he died anyway. It wasn't His will for your daddy to live. From what I know about children falling in wells, it's not going to be His will for that child to get out of the well either."

My mother's face kind of sank. She had a heart for other children. Finally, after what seemed like a long time, Grandmother said, "Well, I don't think they're going to get her out," leaving open the possibility.

I felt some relief at this, and said, "Daddy thinks they can get her out." Grandmother said, "We'll see." I didn't think she believed it, though.

When we got back to the house, I went out to the edge of our yard where there was no grass and the dirt was mostly sand and easy to dig. I used an old spoon my mother had given me to dig a hole as deep as I could, and dropped one of my dollhouse dolls into it.

Daddy came out to get me for lunch and asked, "Are you digging to China?" He didn't see the doll, and I didn't want him to. After he left, I pulled the doll out and brushed her off and told her she was just fine.

Lowell didn't go to the show with us that day. He only liked the movies about cowboys or war, and Jimmy's mother said he could stay at their house while we were gone. So it was only Mother and Daddy and me when we stopped by Mama and Papa's house on our way to the movie later that afternoon. That was fine with me.

As soon as we got out of the car, the air smelled sweet because of the pink azaleas blooming in their yard and you just wanted to take a deep breath and hold it like holding a piece of candy in your mouth to let it melt slow. Mama loved anything pink.

She was sitting in a rocker on the front porch shelling a pan of peas that she had in her lap. The pan was bigger than her lap. "Have you heard any news about Little Kathy Fiscus?" she asked. "We listened about it on the radio this morning, but I had to turn it off, it upset me so bad."

Papa came out and sat down in another rocker. He was a big man, tall and heavy, and slow-moving, while Mama was so short her feet didn't touch the floor when she was in the chair, and hardly weighed enough to get it to rock. My parents stood in front of them, leaning against the porch railings. I went over to the other side of the porch and climbed up on the railing and hoped none of them would look my way because I was not supposed to be standing up there like that.

Mama said, "I feel so sorry for her people. I just can't imagine losing a child down a well, a little child like that."

Papa said, "Maybe they can get her out. I've been thinking about it. I believe if they dug another hole alongside the well and kind of went in from the side..."

My daddy interrupted him. "That's what they're doing, I think." He held up his hands and drew something in the air. "They've been talking about it on the radio this afternoon."

My mother saw me right then and yelled, "Judy! Get off that railing. I have told you a hundred times. Come over here right now!"

I noticed that Papa was smiling a tiny smile. He was trying not to let me see it, though. "Come here," he said to me, and I went and stood in front of his chair. "You watch where you are stepping, now, you hear? Don't want you stepping into no abandoned well. Couldn't do without our Judygirl." He patted me on the back.

***

At the movie, the newsreel was all about Kathy Fiscus. Newsreels were important. Newsreels of Holocaust survivors' release from the death camps had made up my first memory. Even at two and a half years old, standing in the seat next to my mother, leaning into her shoulder, and without much language to attach to what I was seeing, the horror seared itself into my memory and ensured my careful attention to all newsreels I ever saw after that.

While the part about Little Kathy Fiscus was playing, I slid up to sit on the edge of my seat. It was one thing to hear about her on the radio, but another thing to see the real place where she had fallen into the well, and to see so many people gathered around watching. There were big pieces of machinery, and trucks behind the people, and huge lights shining on the ground. I really wanted to see the hole, and look into it, but they didn't show it.

They showed Kathy Fiscus's mother who had the most pitiful face I had ever seen. Then they showed a picture of Little Kathy Fiscus and her sister all dressed up like they were going to a birthday party, and my mother gasped. "She looks like you!" she whispered to me. It was true. As far as I could tell, the girl did look like me—blonde hair with kinky curls, like my hair looked after my mother had rolled it up in pin curls, a big grin, and a face like mine. "She could be your sister," Mother said. I had always wanted a sister.

The movie was a grown-up movie, like most of them, so I spent most of the time thinking about Little Kathy Fiscus down in that dark hole.

The next morning at church, even though it was Easter and we were supposed to be thinking about Jesus rising up out of the tomb, the minister talked on and on about Kathy Fiscus, and about how we "know not the hour nor the day" when Jesus is going to come for us, like he did for her. "The ground could open up at any moment and swallow us up, and we better be ready." My mother had given me a pencil stub, and I pretended I didn't hear what the minister was saying while I drew pictures of rabbits in the margins of the bulletin. I had just learned how to draw rabbits.

By the time we got home from church, it was all over. Daddy and Lowell had stayed home that morning and had been listening to the radio. Daddy motioned to my mother when we came in and called her to the kitchen. Then they came out, and he knelt down to my level.

"Did they get her out?" I asked, because I knew this was about Little Kathy Fiscus.

"Yes, they got her out," Daddy said. "But she didn't make it."

I kept looking at him, because I didn't understand. "She died," he said and put his arm around me. "She's dead," he said for good measure.

"But she's going to be OK, right?" I asked.

My mother sat down on the sofa beside us. She had started taking the pins out of her hat. "They say she died right after she fell in the well."

One more time, I said, "But she'll be OK later, won't she?"

My parents looked at each other. Then my mother said, "Yes, she'll be OK because she is with Jesus now. She'll be fine. But she won't be alive."

My daddy said, "You know, when you remember somebody who died, they are still alive, kind of alive, as long as you remember them."

Later that day, we saw Grandmother Colley when we went to her house for Easter dinner to eat ham and deviled eggs that had little tinges of color on the white part from their starting out being dyed. Lowell wouldn't eat the ones with color on them, and Grandmother made fun of him for being so finicky. Then when she got tired of teasing Lowell about the eggs, she went on to talk about Little Kathy Fiscus and said, "I never thought they had much chance of getting that girl out of the well. All that praying..." She didn't finish her thought.

The next afternoon, when we went over to Mama and Papa's, I saw she had a letter stuck behind the red flag on her mailbox. I always liked to play with the flag, which I did, and saw that the letter was addressed to "The Fiscus Family, San Marino, California."

"Why did you write a letter to those people?" I asked her.

"Just a letter of condolence," she said. "Maybe it'll help. Nothing will really help, though."

Papa said to me, "Don't forget what I told you. Pay attention. Watch where you are going, OK?"

Next Sunday, the preacher was still dwelling on Little Kathy Fiscus. While I drew rabbits, he talked about how sometimes God didn't do what we wanted Him to do, but He's still in charge and we had to accept that "His will be done." It looked like all the people in church felt bad.

The same afternoon, I heard my mother on the phone with her sister. "Poor little girl, never will have the chance to grow up, going to miss her whole life."

At dinner that night, I announced that I was going to remember Little Kathy Fiscus, to keep her alive. My daddy said, "That's fine, but you know that means she will be alive in your heart. No matter how much you remember her, she won't be running around eating fried chicken and playing with her dolls."

"I know," I said.

And I was true to my word. I remembered Little Kathy Fiscus at every turn.

***

Joanie Wilson had surgery to repair her hernia in the summer after Kathy Fiscus fell into the well. The surgery was successful. However, the loss of her hernia made our visits less entertaining after the incision healed. The scar it left was not all that interesting by comparison. Joanie's family moved away from Tifton when we were in the fourth grade. I didn't hear from her again.

Kathy Fiscus never left. She stayed, like a sister, always with me, just one who couldn't get out like I could. She had to live inside me. Since she was going to miss her life, I shared mine with her. It was maybe because of her that I paid such careful attention so I could tell her important things.

When I learned to ride my blue, two-wheeled bicycle, and to pedal as fast as the wind, I told her, "Kathy, this is what it's like to fly a bike."

When I walked barefooted in the springtime through the edge of the shallow pond across from Joanie's house and it was filled with frog eggs and tadpoles, I told her, "Kathy, feel those tadpoles tickling your feet? This is what it's like."

And when the doctor pulled out my tonsils and handed them back to me in a jar, and I got to eat all the ice cream I wanted, I told her about it.

I told her all the rest of it, too. "This is what it's like to read a poem that fills your soul, to paint a picture, to kiss a boy, to graduate from high school, from college, to be in love, to have your heart broken. This is what it's like to be a bride, to hold your sweet baby in your arms, to work and know you've done a good job. This is what it's like to fail, to try again, to climb a mountain, to swim in the ocean, to play with your beautiful grandbaby. This is what it's like."

Margaret

SUMMER 1950

At five years old in 1950, Margaret Callaway was bald as an egg. There was not one hair, not one bit of fuzz to interfere with the shine that made her head glow like the gold-capped dome on the capitol building in Atlanta. I wondered if her mother spit on her head in the morning and polished it with a shoeshine rag. Nobody knew what was the matter with her. She was just bald and you didn't know what to think. Besides her baldness, Margaret was the prettiest little girl you could imagine. She had delicate features, see-through skin, and huge blue eyes with lashes like a movie star. Unfortunately, her blue eyes made the blue veins that ran across her skull even more prominent than they would have been otherwise. Margaret's mother dressed her like Shirley Temple, minus the hair bows, of course. Her dresses had puffed sleeves and full, bouncy skirts tied in the back with oversize sashes. She was never barefooted like the rest of us but wore little, white, unscuffed Mary Janes and white nylon socks trimmed with lace.

The Callaways lived across the street from my grandparents, not that the houses were similar. The Callaways' house was a large Victorian on the corner of Main, a stylish street which their house faced, and 10th, a side street. If you walked out the back door of the Callaways' house and walked across 10th, you would be standing in front of my grandparents' house, a pleasant but modest bungalow. And in 1950, on a summer afternoon, you'd most likely be looking at my grandmother rocking on the porch while she crocheted. Despite the difference in their social standing, Mrs. Callaway and my grandmother, Mama, were friends. Mrs. Callaway frequently came over with Margaret in tow and visited with Mama on the porch. I do not recall Mama ever visiting at the Callaways' house.

My cousin Carol and I were a couple of years older than Margaret. We spent a good bit of time at Mama's house, which was just next door to Carol's. My house was a few blocks away, but we spent no time there. As little girls go, I was more or less the polar opposite of Margaret. In the summertime, I generally wore my brother's handed down shorts and shirts and had on footwear only on Sundays to go to church. If my hair was combed, other than on Sunday, it was because my mother had managed to tackle me in the morning before I headed out for Carol's. Carol did comb her hair and occasionally wore a sundress or sandals.

Carol and I did not give much thought to Margaret. Mama had cautioned us not to stare at her head, or to ever mention the fact that she had no hair. "Mrs. Callaway worries that other children will make fun of her, hurt her feelings," Mama said. For her part, Margaret made it easy not to deal with her because she didn't say a word, nor did she have any expression on her face that indicated a feeling one way or another about anything. She just sat with the women like she was one of them and if she ever saw us, it was like we were another species that held little interest for her.

Apparently, though, Margaret enjoyed her time on Mama's porch to the point that she started crossing the street on her own, and taking up a seat there beside Mama to rock for a while. Mama taught her to crochet, but she never advanced beyond making a long chain, for which there is no earthly purpose, and the activity quickly lost its appeal. Then one afternoon while Carol and I were playing jackstones on the linoleum floor in Mama's kitchen, Mama came back there holding Margaret by the hand.

"Girls," she said, "Margaret would like to play with you. You be nice to her, you hear?" She gave us sharp looks, dropped Margaret's hand, and clicked out of the kitchen back to the porch.

I was on my sevensies, headed to win the game because Carol had not made it past her fivesies. I always did better on Mama's kitchen floor because the linoleum was smooth and even and did not cause the ball to bounce in weird directions like the bumpy hardwood floors did. In addition, it felt cool on our bare legs, and on those summer days, any relief from the heat was welcome.

"Do you want to play jackstones?" I asked, hoping she'd say yes.

"No," Margaret said. "I can't sit on the floor."

"Why not?" Carol asked her.

"It's dirty," Margaret said.

"No, it's not," I said, but Margaret only looked away. "Well, you want to go outside and play *it?*"

"No," Margaret said. "I'd mess up my shoes."

"My goldfish died and we buried him in the sandbox," Carol offered. "We could dig him up and look at him." To which Margaret made no reply.

"I can stand on my head," I said.

"No, you can't," Carol said.

"Do you want to color?" I asked. Mama had some tired old coloring books that had the good pages already colored, but I couldn't think of anything else.

"Yes," Margaret said. "I can stay in the lines very good."

Carol sifted through a bookcase in the hallway and brought out the books and a coffee can that held bits of crayons. She dumped the crayons on the kitchen table with the coloring books and we all sat down. Margaret went right to work with the coloring, but Carol and I lost interest pretty quickly and took the opportunity to look closely at Margaret's head, which brought Mama's china doll to mind.

"Do you know," I asked Margaret, "that Mama has an old, old china doll that she played with when she was a little girl?"

"She won't let us touch it, but sometimes she'll let us look at it. You want to see it?" Carol asked.

Margaret hesitated, but then said, "OK."

The china doll had its own little metal swing, which Mama set up in the middle of the table. She positioned the doll on its seat and gave it a push to set it going. "Y'all just look now. Don't put your hands on her."

After Mama went back out on the porch, I stared at the doll's head, then looked back at Margaret's head. The doll had painted-on shiny black hair. It seemed like a good idea.

"Margaret," I said, "do you like the doll? Do you like her hair?" Margaret eyed me with suspicion. Any mention of hair probably made her wonder what was coming next.

"I guess so," she said.

"I could color some hair on your head like that," I offered.

"No, you couldn't," Carol said.

Margaret didn't know it then, but her future hung in the balance at that moment. She waited a long time, holding on to a blue crayon, and looking back and forth between me and Carol. "No," she said, but there was hesitance in her voice.

I persisted. "It'd be pretty, like Mama's doll."

Margaret looked at the doll and back at me. "You sure?" she asked.

"I can try," I said, "if you really want me to."

Margaret glared at both of us. "My mama would be mad," she said.

"Even if it looks like that?" I asked and pointed at the doll.

"Maybe not," Margaret said. She laid down her crayon, moved her chair over closer to mine, and closed her eyes.

She looked so sweet with those long lashes lying against her pink cheeks that it made me ache to help her. I wanted to be a hero, which I would be if I could help. Unfortunately, like Carol predicted, the crayon didn't work. The color didn't come off on Margaret's head like it did on paper. It hardly even made a mark. Carol inspected my effort, and then said, "Mama's got that old box of water colors. I know where she keeps it."

She went and got the tin paint box from behind the Bab-O under the bathroom sink where Mama had hidden it. We decided on black, like the doll's hair, and I got busy mixing a few drops of water into the dried square of paint with the little brush. When I dabbed some of the paint onto Margaret's head, it seemed for a few minutes like it was going to work. I made swirls that I hoped looked like curls and had an idea that I could even paint on a bow. But then the paint started to drip and run down Margaret's neck and onto her dress.

Carol said, "You're making a mess," and I saw pretty quickly that she was right. There was no way the dripping paint was going to look anything like hair, not even like the hair on the china doll. I was defeated.

"I'm sorry," I told Margaret, trying to find some saving grace. "But, you know, it could be that the paint on your head might make your hair grow."

"That's stupid," Carol said.

We dragged a chair over to the kitchen sink and had Margaret kneel on it with her head under the spigot. I rubbed at the paint on her scalp with a dish towel, but it only smeared and dripped more of it on her face and dress.

Then a strange thing happened. Margaret started giggling. "It tickles," she said. We had never heard her laugh. We had never even seen her smile. At that moment, with black paint streaked all over Margaret's head and down her face, Carol and I knew that we were in big trouble, but hearing Margaret laugh, we started giggling too.

Back then, all the women Mama's age wore oxfords, the kind that laced up and had low heels. You could hear them coming from across the house, clicking out a warning. We were doubled over giggling at the sink with Margaret's paint-smeared head dripping black water down on her yellow dress when we heard the clicks of not just one, but two women. Mrs. Callaway had come over to bring Margaret home. Mama sang out in her high-pitched, tinny voice, "You girls sound like you're having some fun!"

We heard Mrs. Callaway say to Mama, "It's so nice you got Margaret to play with the girls." Then the clicking stopped and they were standing in the kitchen doorway. Mrs. Callaway screeched, "Margaret!"

Mama turned white and collapsed against the table. She had a bad heart. "You girls! What in the world? I can't believe you're doing this. I am so ashamed of you!" She turned to Mrs. Callaway and fell all over herself apologizing, but Mrs. Callaway was busy yanking Margaret out of the chair and telling her what a poor baby she was. She didn't seem to hear any of Mama's pleas.

After the Callaways left, Mama told us to go home, and that she didn't want to see either one of us for the foreseeable future. I have neglected to tell you that Mama had fourteen grandchildren, and that Carol and I were not her favorites. She liked us OK, I guess, but she didn't dote on us like she did some of the others, which would have been a great burden to bear. Of course, she would have had her tongue cut out before she would admit she showed any favoritism among us.

By the time I got back to my house, my mother knew all about what happened and had already gotten out her wooden hair brush, the one she used to spank me. She grabbed my arm and threw me onto my bed on my stomach, which was her preferred position to have me in while she wailed away at my butt and legs. My own tactic was to bite into the quilt on my bed to keep from screaming. It was my way of defying her to not cry for as long as I could hold back. "I don't know what to do with you!" she yelled, over and over. That was what she usually said when she tore into me, and it was right, she didn't, motherless child that she was herself.

***

Later that evening when my daddy came home, I heard mother and him talking in the living room while I was in my room. That was how it always happened. By the time you are seven, you pretty much know who is who and what is what and how all the pieces fit together. She never beat me when he was there, then when he came home, she'd tell him how bad I'd been. Daddy came in to my room. "How you doing, Judygirl? You been upsetting your mother again?"

When I saw him, I started crying and threw myself around his waist. "We were trying to make some hair for Margaret."

He sat down on my bed and held me while he looked up and down my legs for bruises, which he found, but didn't say anything about. "You've got to learn to get along with your mother, now. You know that." Then he asked how we were thinking we could make hair for Margaret, and I told him.

Later, when I was drifting off to sleep, I heard snatches of angry words between my parents. "Bruises on her legs!" and "Won't mind me!" and "I've told you time and again to stop it! She's just a child!" and "Beating!" and "I'm not beating! I'm spanking!" It wasn't new.

A few weeks later, after Mama relented and Carol and I were playing in front of her house, we saw Margaret across the street. "You want to come play?" Carol called to her.

"I can't play with you," Margaret yelled. She was wearing shorts and was barefooted. "My mama won't let me, but I want to show you something."

Carol and I crossed the street to the sidewalk outside the Callaways' fence. "What?" Carol asked.

Margaret dipped her head down toward us. "Look!"

Her head was covered with a fine coat of pale, downy, blonde hair. You had to get right on top of it in the sunlight to see it, but it was there. "Can I touch it?" I asked.

Carol and I both petted Margaret's head, and all of us grinned and giggled until Mrs. Callaway stepped out of the back door and called for Margaret to come inside.

***

Margaret turned six that summer and started school at Annie Belle Clark Elementary School in September with a full head of short, platinum-blonde curls. Carol and I were in third grade that year, but we'd see her sometimes on the playground. We took a proprietary interest in her hair as it grew in thick and curly. It was sad for Mrs. Callaway that just as Margaret fulfilled her dream of a Shirley Temple look-alike daughter, Margaret turned into a tomboy and refused to wear the clothing for the part.

According to Mama, Margaret kept coming across the street to see her from time to time, and Mrs. Callaway allowed the visits as long as Carol and I weren't around.

Larry

FALL 1950

"He's a social promotion," I said to Mrs. Cochran, the substitute teacher for Mrs. Oscar Burkett's third-grade class. Larry Horn sat way in the rear of the room, pushed back even from the last row of desks because he smelled bad, because he didn't bathe, and his clothes were dirty. He was ten years old and a head taller than the rest of us. His habit was to come into class in the morning, answer roll call, say the Lord's Prayer and the Pledge of Allegiance, and then lay his head on his desk and sleep until lunchtime. At lunchtime, he rallied long enough to eat his free lunch before returning to his nap. During recess, he hung around one of the loblolly pine trees in the playground by himself kicking dirt with his too-small shoes with the toes cut out. Mrs. Burkett never called on him. She had tried early in the school year but not anymore. Finally she gave up and now she just let him sleep.

Mrs. Cochran came in to substitute after Mrs. Oscar Burkett broke into a sob in the middle of working out a long division problem on the blackboard, still holding on to a piece of chalk in one hand and the eraser in the other. She was going through a DIVORCE, the first one I had ever heard of. Maybe it was the shame of it, or maybe Mr. Oscar Burkett had done something that made her feel bad, and she started to cry and ran out of the room. We kids looked at one another. The boys began to giggle after a while. Some of the girls teared up. Then Mrs. Marks, the principal, came in. "I'll be your teacher today!" she announced like it was going to be a barrel of fun. It was soon clear that while she might be a good principal (our parents said so), she didn't know diddly about teaching. She found Mrs. Burkett's *Tom Sawyer* and spent the rest of the day reading to us, which was entertaining enough, but we knew it was not teaching. I was glad to see Mrs. Cochran come in to substitute the next day.

I loved Mrs. Cochran. She was the oldest person I knew and wore her white hair in a bun at the back of her head and long black skirts that reached almost to the floor, and she smelled sweet, like baby powder. She had substituted for us in second grade from time to time and had taught most of our parents when they were our age. She called us Mr. This and Miss That. It made you want to sit up a little straighter when she said, "Miss Ireland, will you tell us what you have learned about amphibians?" I wanted to please her, so I appointed myself her helper whenever she substituted, telling her the way things were, so to speak, which is how I came to tell her he's "a social promotion," about Larry. I guess I thought those few words summed up the entirety of Larry Horn so that Mrs. Cochran would know how to deal with him. Mrs. Cochran, however, would have none of it.

"What does that mean, 'social promotion'?" She frowned at me.

"Well," I said, "he couldn't pass second grade, and they just let him come on up to third because he was getting a lot bigger than the other kids. They call it social promotion."

"I know what social promotion is, Miss Ireland," she said. "What I do not know is why social promotion means he should not participate in the class." There was an edge to her voice, and I understood why. Even though we kids never talked about it, I think we all knew that it wasn't right, Larry sitting at a desk way away from the rest of the class and just being there, but not really being there, like a ghost or something. We went to Sunday school. We knew it wasn't right, and underneath, we felt bad for Larry. At least I did.

When recess came, Mrs. Cochran walked back to Larry's desk while the rest of us filed out to the playground. I watched her put her hand on his shoulder and heard her say quietly, "You stay, Mr. Horn. I'd like to speak with you."

When we returned from recess, Larry was sitting up at his desk with a book open in front of him, and his face and hands were clean for a change. I noticed that the apple that had been on Mrs. Cochran's desk was gone.

It took Mrs. Oscar Burkett two weeks to get over the effects of the DIVORCE enough to return to teaching. All during that time, Larry Horn sat up in his desk and held the correct book open with clean hands and face, even though he still smelled bad. Mrs. Cochran taught as usual except several times a day she took strolls back to Larry's desk, pointing at places in his book, and at recess, Larry stayed in the room with her. I envied him, all that attention from her.

After Mrs. Burkett came back to school, and Mrs. Cochran disappeared into whatever her life was when she wasn't teaching, Larry continued to sit up, rather than lay his head down, for about another week. Then, gradually, he went back to sleep and quit washing his face and hands, and the old order returned.

***

The biggest event on the Annie Belle Clark Elementary School calendar was the annual Halloween carnival. Mrs. Burkett had only recently returned from her absence when we started getting ready for it.

My mother had been busy for weeks making clothespin dolls to donate to the PTA craft booth. She had a talent for sewing, and the dolls were something to behold. She took regular stick-type clothespins, the ones that already look like a person with a round head and two legs. She painted lovely little faces and shoes on them, and made arms from pipe cleaners she wrapped in pink ribbon. She gathered fabric bits into full skirts and created bodices from more scraps of fabric and lace and ribbons. She made hair from embroidery floss and hats from starched pieces of cloth and feathers and sequins. She made dozens of them, each one more beautiful than the last.

"Can I have this one?" I asked her about one with a navy velvet skirt and lace petticoat, blue-jay feathers in her hair.

"No," she said. "They're for the carnival."

"Well, how about this one?" I held up one with a green satin skirt and pink ribbon rosettes around the edge of her shawl.

"Quit asking. After the carnival, if there are any left, you can have one."

The carnival was always on Saturday night, no matter what day of the week Halloween fell on, so we could stay up late and have fun and not worry about school the next day. Miss Anne Burkett, the other third-grade teacher, turned her classroom into a haunted house every year, with all the lights out and bowls of spaghetti to feel in the dark while she told you it was dead people's brains, and marbles in Jell-O that she said were eyeballs, and somebody's father who jumped out at you at the end yelling "boo." There were games of chance, no matter that the Baptists didn't think they were moral, where you could pay a nickel and pick out from a washtub a floating rubber duck that had a number on its bottom to show which tiny toy or piece of bubble gum you won. There was a costume contest at the end of the night, last thing, and prizes for the best ones. My mother had made harlequin suits for me and Lowell that year, orange and black with a big ruffle around the neck, but we only won honorable mention.

It was all safe and, like I said, 1950, so we had the run of the school to ourselves during the carnival, the familiar rooms and wooden floors scrubbed with smelly sawdust wax turned like magic into an exotic place by the late hour, and the crepe paper draped from the ceiling and the booths set up all along the corridors. I kept an eye on the PTA craft booth where my mother sat with another mother to sell the dolls and aprons and pot holders and slingshots (which could blind you if you weren't careful). They also had baked goods for sale, and a cakewalk. I zeroed in on the dolls, which were disappearing at an alarming rate.

Larry Horn, who never came to anything outside of class, was there with his little sister, a first grader. He kept hold of her hand the whole time and treated her with such tenderness that it was touching, particularly as we had not seen him this way before. Their only costumes were buckram eye masks, a white one for her and a black one for him. He paid the nickel for her to pick out a rubber duck, and she won a Chinese finger puzzle, but that was all I saw them do. Most of us had been given a couple of dollars, which let us play the majority of the games.

After the costume contest, I walked back to the PTA booth, hoping at least one of the dolls would be left. My mother pointed to the doll display where the doll with the blue plaid skirt and the yellow lace bodice remained. It wasn't my favorite, but still, I was happy that I'd get to keep it.

Right then, Larry and his sister walked up, Larry still clutching her hand like he was afraid someone was going to snatch her away from him. "This is Bernice," he said.

I nodded. I wanted them to leave. The carnival was over. My mother and the other woman were packing the remaining stuff so we could go home. My mother picked up the doll to put it in her box when Bernice's eyes lit up like a streetlight. "Can I hold it?" she asked.

Larry pulled her away. "We don't have money for that, Bernie," he whispered loud enough for us to hear him. He tried to turn her around, but she would not be moved.

"I just want to touch it. Please," she begged.

You had to admit, even dirty as she was, the little girl was cute as all get out. Mother leaned down and smiled at Bernice. "Sure, you can hold it, honey," she said, and handed her the doll. I always knew that she had wanted a little girl with black curls like Bernice, when what she got was towheaded me. That was just part of how we were together.

Bernice's eyes got even bigger. She took the doll and held it against her heart and kissed it. My mother looked at me. She didn't have to say out loud that she wanted me to give the doll to Larry's sister. She was always trying to get me to do the right thing, whether or not I felt like it. If it had been the doll with the rose-colored skirt and the pink feathers, I'd not have done it, but as it was the plaid one, I shrugged my shoulders and said, "She can have it." Bernice almost cried, but I was still not happy about the forced generosity.

The next Monday, Larry did not come to school. That afternoon, my daddy, who was a mailman and knew everything that happened in town, told us that the Horn's house had burned to the ground, nothing left of what little they had to begin with. Everyone agreed it was one of the saddest things they had ever heard of, and we should try to be nice to Larry. On Tuesday, when Larry came back, kids at school who had never said a word to him said, "I'm sorry about your house" when they passed by. When I saw him, I asked him if Bernice's doll got burned up. He looked down and said, "All of it got burned."

When I told my mother about the doll, she went straight to the closet where she kept her Singer sewing machine and set it up on the kitchen table. She found a clothespin and got to work making a new doll for Bernice. When she finished, she gave it to me to take to Larry at school.

"I don't want to," I told her. "You didn't make one for me. You said you would, but you didn't."

My mother grabbed me by the arm and shook me. "You are the most selfish thing I have ever known!" she said. "How would you feel if all your dolls and toys and clothes got burned up?"

My mother put the doll in a paper sack, so Larry wouldn't have to feel unmanly or something carrying it around. I waited until recess and went over to his tree and handed it to him. "My mother made this for Bernice," I said.

He looked in the sack and smiled. "She'll be glad to get it," he said. "Thank you."

"It's not from me," I explained. "It's from my mother."

"Do you want to go on the swings?" he asked.

I said, "No. Like I said, the doll is from my mother." That was what I was afraid of, that Larry would think I wanted to be his friend, and that the other kids would see me with him. Bad as I felt for him, I didn't want to make that sacrifice.

When I caught up with Sally Ann and her jump rope, she said, "Is Larry your new boyfriend?" in a sneering way, just like I figured she would do.

***

My daddy was in the American Legion. Almost all the fathers had been in the war, and now that they were home and the war was over, they put on their Legion hats and badges and marched in the parades. They did other stuff too, like take boxes of food to needy families at the holidays. My daddy was set to take boxes to three families that Thanksgiving. When I came home from school the day before Thanksgiving, he was loading the boxes in the trunk of our old black Ford.

"Can I come with you?" I asked. I wanted to go anywhere he went, and usually he let me.

"You have to promise to stay in the car and wait for me when I go into their houses."

"I'm taking one of these boxes to the Horns, that boy in your class. He doesn't need to see you, you hear?"

I agreed. I didn't want him to see me any more than he might have wanted to see me.

"Mr. Medford's letting the Horns stay in one of his old tenant-farmer houses since the fire. Shack, more like it. Don't even know if there's running water out there."

Two of the families lived in the housing projects, which were just on the edge of town. The car was close enough that I could see when Daddy went up to the first house and a bedraggled looking woman came to the door with a baby in her arms and two little kids hanging on either side of her dress. She cried when he showed her the box that was so full a big old ham was sticking out of it. I couldn't see to the other house.

To get to the Horns' we drove out into the country through fields of brown stubble from the spent crops. That's fall in South Georgia, not beautiful leaves on trees like we saw in our picture books at school, just brown stubble in the fields. Eventually, Daddy turned onto a bumpy dirt road and we went a little way before he pulled over and parked. The driveway, if you could call it that, was up ahead. He pointed out the house, which was, as he said, more like a shack, unpainted and leaning to one side. I could see well enough to see a man in overalls open the front door. I thought about lying down in the seat so there'd be no way for Larry to see me, but I didn't. Much as I didn't want him to know I was there, it was a little like looking at a scab on somebody's knee, where it was gross but you wanted to see it anyway.

Daddy walked up to the edge of the porch carrying the box. Mr. Horn didn't come out of the door. He just stood there. Finally, Daddy set the box on the porch then stuck out his hand and held it there until Mr. Horn came out and shook his hand.

While all this was going on and I was peeking over the bottom of the window, I saw Larry come around from the back of the house, hunkered down and walking low to the ground like he thought he was hiding. He was heading toward our car, but then he stopped and crouched behind some privet hedges.

Daddy finished his business and strode back to the car and got in. Mr. Horn lifted his box of food into the house and closed the door. I was about to tell Daddy about Larry when there was a loud crack of something hitting the side of the car. I was startled and slid over toward Daddy. He patted me on the back. "It's OK," he said, and we got a glimpse of Larry hightailing it back to the house.

"The boy just threw a rock at us," Daddy said, like it was something surprising but also a wonder. He got out and walked around the car to look at the place where the rock had hit. He rubbed at it for a minute and then got back in and cranked up the car.

"Are you going to tell his daddy?" I asked.

"I think that man's got enough on his plate right now, don't you?" he said. "And the boy's had a hard enough life. We don't need to add to it. I guess throwing a rock at us was all he knew to do."

I thought about this while he got the car turned around and we headed home.

"Have I had a hard life?" I asked.

He looked at me. He knew what I was thinking about. It took him a while to answer. "You have some differences with your mother that I wish you didn't have, for sure, but lined up against what that boy has had to deal with, you're doing OK."

That cheered me, lifted me out of feeling sorry for myself, which I could do when I thought about Carol's mother, who held her and loved on her and hardly ever raised her voice. My mother believed sparing the rod meant spoiling the child. And even when I wasn't doing something bad, she held me at arm's length. She thought it was babying children to hug and kiss them, and that it would keep them from turning into good, strong, Christian people when they got to be older.

***

Larry didn't come back to school after Thanksgiving. The week before Christmas, Daddy told us he had seen Mr. Horn in town and he told him that the family had come into some good luck. His uncle had died in North Georgia and had left them a farm up around Summerville, and they were getting ready to leave Tifton.

I thought about Larry going to a new school and wondered if he would go into the third grade again, or if he'd not say he was a social promotion and just take up a new life in the fifth grade where he was supposed to be. I hoped he would start bathing and that he'd do better, that his new life wouldn't be so hard. I don't know what actually did happen with him. We never heard from the Horns after they left. I took that as good news.

As for my own hard life, I figured it could have been worse. My daddy was right.

Sally Ann
WINTER 1950

"Don't be scared, honey," Andi said to me. I said I wasn't scared, but I was. I was always scared going up that dark stairway behind the Andersons' kitchen. "Those guys up there just got themselves into a bit of trouble with the law," she continued. "They wouldn't hurt a fly." Andi was Sally Ann's mother, a sweet lady, always smiling, and tall and stout. She walked leaning forward, like she was eager to meet anyone coming her way, and was willing to go farther than half the distance between the two of you to make it happen. She wouldn't let anybody call her Miss Andi or Mrs. Anderson. "I'm just Andi," she said, even when my mother tried to make me call her Mrs. Anderson, like I had to with every other adult lady. Even Sally Ann and Buddy, her own children, called her Andi.

Sally Ann's daddy was the sheriff of Tift County, and her family lived in the jailhouse. That is, Sally Ann and her brother, and her mother and daddy lived on the bottom floor of the big old box of a redbrick building, and the prisoners were housed on the second floor. The stairway between the kitchen and the back door led up to the jail, which was a wide hallway lined with six cells, three on each side. A scratched-up old desk and a straight chair were at the far end of the hallway. Most times, only three or four cells were occupied.

Andi did the cooking for the prisoners whom she fed whatever she fed her family. My mother complained that the Andersons didn't have to pay for their house or their groceries because the county paid for all of it, while food was expensive and we had to pay good money for every bite we put in our mouths.

When you spent the night with Sally Ann, which was spooky enough just knowing that the prisoners were sleeping right upstairs from where you were laying down your own head, you had to help bring them their dinner. Andi would arrange their plates on trays on the kitchen table and load them up. She was a good cook, and she took care to make the plates look nice. If something was blooming in the yard, she'd pick little flowers and put them on the trays. Then, whoever was around would be called on to carry one of the trays up the stairs with her.

That's what scared me, going up those dark stairs. And even though you'd be going up, not down, it felt like going into hell, with the men in their raggedy striped suits, unshaven and missing teeth, crouching in the corners on their cots or peering out through the bars with their hungry eyes. I knew they couldn't hurt me, locked up as they were, but just being in that close to them meant rubbing up against a bleaker world and having to face the fact that a place filled with such misery was out there.

At the top of the stairs, Andi unlocked the door to the cell block and sang out, "Dinner time, gentlemen!" Sally Ann and I trailed in behind her with our trays while Andi began greeting each one of them.

"Mr. Allen, how are you this evening? I hope you like fried chicken. Mr. Jackson, Sheriff Anderson said he's going to come up and talk with you later on tonight." Then she took the trays and passed them one by one through slots in the bars. "Wait now," she said. "You know we have to say the blessing."

After all the trays had been distributed, she asked, "Who wants to say grace?" After a lot of mumbling and head shaking, Andi said, "Let's all bow our heads," and she checked to see that everyone in the room obeyed the command before she asked God to bless the food to the nourishment of our bodies and us to His service, and to forgive us of our sins. It made me wonder what sins the men were thinking of while they were asking for forgiveness.

We got to leave after the grace with the prisoners and go downstairs for our own dinner. You'd think it might have spoiled my appetite, scared as I was, but it didn't. It had just the opposite effect. I felt relieved that I could reenter a world where we had all our teeth and clean clothes, and life was generally good. When I was at Sally Ann's, I ate like it was my last opportunity to take in nourishment in this life.

After we finished our meal and took our dishes off the table, we had to go back to collect the plates from the men upstairs. They always handed the plates to us through the slots as polite as could be, and said how it was good, and "thank you," but my imagination still got away with me, thinking about ways they could do us harm if they wanted to, like fling their plates at us or spit in our faces or something.

My mother's view of Sally Ann was that she was "spoiled rotten." "Andi lets that child get away with murder," she said. Of course, my mother said that about several of my friends, including Carol. Where Sally Ann was concerned, I understood what she meant. Sally Ann sometimes just said "yes" when she answered her mother, rather than saying "yes, ma'am." If I'd said "yes" to my mother, I'd have gotten a smack across my rear end. Andi only asked, "What did you say?" over and over until Sally Ann said "yes, ma'am." Sally Ann also talked back to her mother in other ways I knew would have gotten me spanked until I couldn't sit down. The reason I got to play with Sally Ann at all was that Andi and my mother were friends in the Eastern Star, and if I hadn't been allowed to visit Sally Ann, it would have been hard for my mother to explain to Andi. So when I was with Sally Ann, I was often filled with wonder at some of what went on between her and Andi.

A few weeks before Christmas, I was playing at Sally Ann's house. Two huge live oak trees dripping with Spanish moss stood in the side yard, and Sheriff Anderson had tied a couple of swings to them. We were swinging, laughing, having a good time, when Sally Ann started dragging her shoes through the dirt under the swing every time it slowed down. We all wore brown and white saddle oxfords, and she had gotten the white part on hers filthy.

"You're messing up your shoes," I told her.

"I want some new ones," she said. "If I can ruin these, Andi will take me to get new ones."

"My mother would jerk a knot in me if I did that," I said.

Right then, Sheriff Anderson showed up alongside the tree. We hadn't heard him or seen him, but there he was, sharp in his khaki uniform and his silver star and his gun belt, his hands on his hips. "Sally Ann." he yelled. "Stop that this minute! Get in the house and get those shoes cleaned and polished. Now! Don't think you're going to get any new pair of shoes in the next year or so either, not till your toes turn black and blue from being cramped in the ones you have on."

Sally Ann nearly fell off the swing. Sheriff Anderson made up for Andi's looseness in child-rearing.

"Yes, sir," she said. "I'm sorry." But she wasn't.

Sheriff Anderson got into his car (another thing that the county paid for that my mother resented) and cranked it up. He stuck his head out of the window before he drove off. "You better have those shoes polished and sitting by the door for me to see when I get home, young lady!" Then he pulled out of the yard without looking at us again.

I followed Sally Ann into the house. We were there alone. Andi was with my mother at a PTA meeting, and I don't know where Buddy was. Sally Ann found the shoe polish, brown paste and white liquid, and a rag, and spread out a newspaper on the kitchen floor. She scrubbed at one shoe. "I hate my daddy," she said.

Sally Ann often said things that struck me so hard I didn't have any words to come back with, and this was one of those times. At my house, we were preached at to never say "hate" about anybody, and this was her daddy she said she hated! After the littlest bit of time working on the shoe, she said, "I know what I'm going to do." She gathered up the shoe polish and rag and her shoes, and said, "Come on with me. We're going upstairs. I'm going to make old Joe clean my shoes. He polished my daddy's one time."

The first thing Andi ever told us about their house was that we were never, never, ever to go upstairs to the jail unless she or the sheriff was with us. That was no problem for me. I'd have never gone up there, period, if it were left to me. "We can't go up there," I said. "Your mother and daddy aren't here to go with us. I promised Andi. And you don't have the key."

Sally Ann gave me her sneer, which she was good at. "You're a fraidy-cat, and I know where the key is."

I was not a fraidy-cat. I was hardly afraid of anything, but I was afraid of going up those stairs. "No I'm not!" I said. "But I'm not stupid."

Sally Ann stuffed her shoes, the polish and rag, and a piece of newspaper in a grocery bag and headed for the stairs. "You coming or not?"

Much as I didn't want to go upstairs, I didn't want her to go by herself either. And I didn't want her to think I was afraid. Sally Ann could do some real damage to my standing with the other girls in Mrs. Oscar Burkett's third-grade class, and she'd do it without a second thought. She could be mean as a snake, which was part of her appeal. You never knew what Sally Ann would do, but you wanted to be there to see it.

She got the key off a hook in the kitchen and headed up the stairs. I followed behind her step by step. She didn't hesitate a second, which made me wonder if she came up here all the time by herself.

After she opened the door at the top of the stairs, I went in after her and plastered my back against it to wait for Sally Ann to do what she was going to do. Most of the time, there would be three or four men in the jail. But that day, it was only old Joe Collins. He was in the jail about half the time, it seemed like. "Hard to be a drunk in a dry county," my daddy said about Joe. I don't know what he did besides public drunkenness, but it must have been something bad to get him in there so much.

Sally Ann walked right up to his cell and stuck her dirty shoes through the slot that Andi slipped the dinner plate in. "I want you to clean my shoes, Joe," she said. "Here's a wet rag to clean them, and some white and some brown polish. You need anything else?"

Old Joe just looked at the shoes but didn't touch them. "Where's your mama, Sally Ann?"

I piped up, out of nervousness or maybe out of fine training for eight years to always answer any adult who asks you a question. "She's at PTA with my mother."

Sally Ann's eyebrows shot up and she glared at me. "But my daddy's just downstairs. He's reading the paper. He'll be up any minute now."

Old Joe grinned. "You too good at lying, little missy. Don't you know I heard your daddy drive off in the sheriff vehicle about half an hour ago? I could pick out the rumble of that engine from among a dozen cars. And I ain't heard him come driving back since he left."

Sally Ann decided not to respond to Joe's accusation. "You can clean my shoes. You aren't doing anything else I can see."

"What'll you give me if I do?" Joe asked.

"I won't give you anything!" Sally Ann said.

"Then you can take your nasty old shoes and polish them yourself," Joe said. He sat down on his cot and picked up a magazine.

"Let's go downstairs," I said. "I'll help you clean your shoes."

"No," Sally Ann said. "Look, Joe, I'll give you a nickel."

"What am I supposed to do with a flat nickel?" Joe asked. "You give me fifty cents and I'll do it."

"I don't have fifty cents," Sally Ann said.

"OK." Joe said. He took the shoes and the polish and put them on the floor at the far corner of his cell. "I tell you what, missy. You go find that fifty cents and bring it to me, and I'll do the shoes. If you don't, I'll show your daddy your shoes and tell him about you coming up here."

43

"He won't believe you," Sally Ann said.

"Where's he going to think I got these dirty old shoes?" Joe asked, grinning. "And you remember I said I'm going to tell your daddy, not your sweet mama."

Sally Ann put her hands on her hips and gave Joe her dirtiest look. "You're an old skunk!" she yelled.

"Let's go," I whispered to Sally Ann. I wanted to get out of there.

She stomped down the stairs. "We've got to find some money," she said. I dragged behind as she went from room to room searching through drawers and on top of dressers, shaking coins out of Buddy's tin monkey bank and her own piggy bank. She came up with the fifty cents after about half an hour, but she was fuming mad. "That's all my allowance money," she said. "I'm not going to get to go to the show on Saturday! And Buddy is going to know something's not right when he checks his monkey bank. He'll tell."

We went back up the stairs, and Sally Ann dumped the coins through the slot in Joe's cell. "There you go!" she said. "Now clean my shoes like you said."

Joe took his time counting out the fifty cents. Then, calm as a cucumber, he pushed Sally Ann's dirty shoes and the polish back through the slot.

"I gave you the money," she said. "Now polish them!"

"No, ma'am," Old Joe said. "You got a lot of lessons to learn, little lady."

"I hate you!" Sally Ann said. She reached up to get her shoes, and that's when Joe clamped his hairy old hand on top of hers, and wrapped his fingers around her wrist, and she screamed, "Let me go!" I was hanging onto the doorknob as tight as I could, ready to jerk it open.

"Your little friend over there is about to wet her pants." Old Joe laughed. He was right. He held onto Sally Ann, who had started to cry. I just trembled.

"Here's your first lesson, Miss Sally Ann," he said. "Don't you ever come up here again unless you are with your mama or your daddy. You hear me? A lot of these guys that wind up here aren't as nice as me. They'd break your arm just as soon as not. You messing with stuff you don't want to mess with coming up here. You hear me?"

Sally Ann screamed, "Yes! Let me go!"

Old Joe said, "What did you say?"

44

"Yes, sir!" she said, and Joe let go.

Sally Ann jerked her arm away. I held the door open, and she ran down the stairs. I saw the key on the desk way at the end of the room and knew I had to get it to lock the door. Before, I'd have been scared silly to walk all that way between the cells, but somehow, I didn't feel afraid anymore.

After I picked up the key and was going back to the door, Joe called to me. "Hey, little friend. Miss Judy!"

I froze. Having him say my name felt like he had broken into my house and was staring at me.

"Yes, sir?" I said.

"I got a lesson for you too. Don't you let Miss Sally Ann lead you down no garden path. You got to think for your own self about stuff when you with her. You hear me?"

"Yes, sir," I said.

I went out and locked the door. When I got back down the stairs, Sally Ann was red-faced and spitting mad, busy spreading out newspaper on the kitchen floor again to clean her shoes.

* * *

Sally Ann and I went separate ways after elementary school, as much as it's possible to go separate ways when your cohort is barely over a hundred people to begin with. She was a cheerleader in high school and was popular. She won the "prettiest" category in the voting for superlatives our senior year. She married a lawyer from a suburb of Atlanta, and I heard they did well financially. Our only direct communication after high school consisted of hellos and how-are-yous at the reunions, which she attended as regularly as I did. That was it. Then during the picnic at the fiftieth, out of nowhere she took me by the arm, pulled me aside, and said, with authority in her voice, "Your hair is too long. You need to get it cut." I was stunned and nearly reacted with something snarky but got hold of myself before I did. When I looked at her and realized how perfectly put together she was, I understood she was offering me a gift, something from her world to mine. "Thank you," I said. "I will tell my hairdresser as soon as we get back to California. I appreciate your pointing that out to me." I meant it. We all do what we can do.

Baby

SUMMER 1951

Rosa Parsons was the one Mama or Aunt Ethelle called on when they needed extra help for things, like Aunt Ethelle getting overcome with housecleaning, what with four children running around making messes, or Mama not being able to do her housework when she was feeling weak from her bad heart. My mother called Rosa, too, but only rarely, when she was desperate, like if she got so far behind with the ironing that we didn't have anything to wear that wasn't in the ironing basket. My mother thought that there was something shameful about a woman not doing her own housework and would slave away into the night to keep from admitting she needed assistance, while Mama and Aunt Ethelle had no problem at all with having someone come in to give them a break.

Mama had known Rosa forever. Rosa had helped her with the last three of her five children when they were little. She was younger than Mama, but not by much—a tall, thin black woman who had graying hair pulled into two knots at the back of her head. Addie Mae was Rosa's daughter, and Baby was Addie Mae's little girl. When Baby was only a year old, Addie Mae ran off to Chicago and left Baby with Rosa. Addie Mae came home on the train every Christmas with lots of presents, saying she was going to take Baby to Chicago with her just as soon as she could. Baby was eight years old, but she hadn't seen the inside of the train yet.

Carol and I were about the same age as Baby, and the summer this happened, Carol had just turned nine, and Baby and I were still eight. When Baby was a baby, and after Addie Mae left, Rosa brought her with her any time she came to work. Mama would let my mother know that Rosa was coming with Baby, and she would drop me off at Mama's house for Rosa to watch along with Carol and Baby while she did her work. Rosa said she could keep an eye on three children as well as one, and that we entertained each other and made it easy. Carol and I loved playing with Baby. She was sweet and funny. She knew games and songs and kept us laughing. She had dark brown skin and hair in little braids all over her head. When Baby got to be five, Rosa stopped bringing her. "Y'all getting big now," she said. She had a neighbor lady who could watch her then.

Somebody had to drive out to Phillipsburg to pick up Rosa and bring her into town when she was needed, and it was often my daddy who made the trip. On the morning Daddy told me Mama wanted him to pick up Rosa, and that Baby would be coming too because the lady who usually watched her was away, I was excited about it because we hadn't seen her in so long. He dropped me off at Mama's before he drove out to get Rosa and Baby. He never took me with him to Phillipsburg.

Carol and I were in shorts and shirts and barefooted, the way we usually were in the summer, but Baby arrived in a red plaid dress with a big white collar and sandals. Rosa always kept her looking fancy. She had gotten taller in the couple of years since we had last seen her, and we had too, like we were more grown up, so at first we felt a little strange. Then Baby took off her sandals to be more like us, and we were the same again. Baby was good at knowing what to do.

Mama sat all of us down when Baby got there and told us we'd have to keep out of the house because she and Rosa had work to do. The Harmons, who lived out in the country and had a garden, had given her a bushel of beans, a great big box of tomatoes, and two baskets of peaches. She and Rosa were going to can the tomatoes and beans and make jam out of the peaches. They'd be using the pressure cooker, and we couldn't be anywhere near the kitchen because it was liable to blow up and kill everybody. Children were not even allowed in the house while the pressure cooker was on the stove. Why the women would willingly lay a hand on that deadly pot just to put some beans and tomatoes in jars was beyond my ability to understand.

Mama also told us that we were to stay in the backyard. Rosa jumped in to emphasize Mama's words. "The backyard. Not the front yard, the backyard!" Thin as she was, Rosa had a sturdier build than Mama and was a different creature altogether from Mama. While Mama fussed at us, her words were not supported by any action, and she usually got over being mad at us within a few minutes, in an hour at most, and it was clear she had an underlying affection for us even if we weren't her favorites. Rosa was not held back by gentle affection, not for us nor for Baby either, that I could see. She kept her angry face long after we committed any offense, and she was apt to yank you up by your arm and give it a quick shake that made you think it was coming out of the socket. You didn't want to get on Rosa's bad side.

Rosa and Mama had a strong bond between them. We didn't know what all of it was about, but one thing they shared was a belief that neither one of them got the respect due them as mothers and grandmothers. Mama talked a good bit about how Rosa had not brought Addie Mae up to do her like she did—having that baby out of wedlock and running away to Chicago—and Rosa certainly didn't deserve for Addie Mae to leave Baby with her to bring up.

Carol and I agreed that no one deserved Baby. Having Baby left with you would be a pure sign of the grace of God, a gift that no one deserved. We knew from Sunday school about the grace of God. We knew that none of us even deserved the sunshine or the air we breathed, and that it was only through the grace of God that we had them. So how could anybody deserve Baby?

Likewise, we had often overheard Rosa complaining about one or another of our aunts or uncles that Mama felt had not paid enough attention to her needs, particularly with her bad heart. And if Rosa was around when Carol and I didn't hop to at the very minute Mama told us to do something, Rosa yelled at us. "Didn't you hear your grandma calling you? Are you deaf?" Mama appreciated Rosa taking up for her. "Y'all listen to Rosa, now, and mind what she says."

After we got our instructions from Mama and Rosa to keep ourselves busy in the backyard, Carol and Baby and I played chase. Baby was way faster than either of us. She was kind, though, and offered us tips on getting faster, like taking deep breaths and swinging your arms while you ran. Then we played hide-and-go-seek. I was always the best at hiding, in any group, to the point that the other kids often gave up and started playing another game among themselves while I was still crumpled up inside a cardboard box or lying flat on the corrugated tin roof of a shed and hadn't heard them yell, "All in free!" That day, I went into a closet in the garage that we had been sworn never to enter because it contained Papa's secret Mason things, and he'd have to die if we saw them. I knew they'd never look there. It was boiling hot in the closet, though, so I came out on my own as soon as I could hear the commotion of them looking for me settle down.

"We're reading the library books," Carol said when I came out of the garage. They were sitting on the bench under the pecan tree with books spread out on the picnic table. Carol and I had already read the books. Baby had finished two Bobbsey Twins and a couple of the picture books.

"That was nice," she said. "We don't have a library in Phillipsburg. We got one at school, but school's out, so I don't have nothing new to read until September."

My mouth dropped open from the very idea of it. It may have been the first time Carol and I got a true glimpse of the world from someone else's eyes, trying to imagine what it would have been like to not have a library. The Tift County library was important to us. It occupied one of the sprawling old Victorians on Ridge Avenue, the one on the corner of 12th Street that the Stevenson family had donated to the city, and was only a block and a half away from Mama's house. We trotted up there a couple of times a week to check out books and return the ones we'd read. The children's section was in the large foyer, as were the librarian's desk and the librarian herself, Mrs. Mitchell, who was strict about her rules and made us show her our hands so she could see that they were clean before we picked up the books.

When Baby told us there was no library in Phillipsburg, Carol said, "Well, you can read ours. We can go to the library right now and get some new ones. We can keep on reading until you have to go home this afternoon." It felt like little to offer, but it was all we had.

Even before we learned about the absence of a library in Phillipsburg, Carol and I knew that Baby's lot in life was different from ours in fundamental ways, but it wasn't something that we thought much about. We knew she had to drink from a different water fountain at the Belk department store, the one that said, "Colored Only." And we knew that she sat in the balcony at the Tift Theater to see movies, while we couldn't sit there. And we knew that when we were in the back seats of our cars riding through the country in the late summer and saw people bent over picking cotton, it was only black people like her doing it. It was just the way it was. So, some of the differences between us were right there in front of us, whether we thought about them or not. I wondered how much Baby thought about them.

"How we going to go to the library when Miss Tennie said to stay in the backyard?" Baby asked.

Carol and I looked at each other. Then Carol said, "I know how. We can go from Mama's backyard to my backyard, and cross the street and go into the Hardys' backyard. We'll be out of backyards for a little way right there crossing the street, but it's not far. Then we go from the Hardys' backyard through the privet hedge into Misses Lovey and Sweet's backyard, and over to the library's backyard!"

Baby said, "Miss Tennie meant her backyard, not just anybody's backyard."

It was clear that Carol and I were more used to breaking rules, or at least, twisting them to our purposes. "She just said the backyard," I said. "It's almost the same. Anyway, it won't take long. We can be back before they know we ever left."

Baby finally got persuaded, and we took off, me carrying all our books from last week while Carol held Baby's hand. Everything went fine until I popped out on the other side of the hedge that separated the Hardys' yard from Misses Lovey and Sweet's.

Lovey and Sweet Davis were maiden lady sisters who had grown up with Papa. They were that old. "Neither one of them ever even had a boyfriend that I know of," he'd said one time. They lived in the old Victorian they had shared with their parents until the parents died. Now it was just the two of them living there, "while the house crumbles around them," Papa said.

When I crawled into their backyard, there was Miss Sweet hanging up tea towels on the clothesline. She saw me as soon as I stood up. Carol and Baby were behind me and hadn't yet come through the hedge. We hadn't expected Lovey and Sweet to be outside, hot as it was, but I guess you had to dry your tea towels no matter about the heat.

"Hey!" Miss Sweet called out. "What are you doing under my privet hedge? You're a little Ireland, aren't you?" Our towheads were dead giveaways. The thing about Sweet and Lovey was that if you ever got waylaid by them, you were stuck. They loved to talk, and you'd be trapped until kingdom come trying to figure out some way to get free of them and still be nice. Carol was right behind me. When she stood up, Miss Sweet said, "You're another one of the Irelands!" Then Baby crawled out and Miss Sweet said, "You're not an Ireland!" and laughed, like that was real funny.

By this time, Miss Lovey, who had been watching from the back porch, walked out in the yard. "Who's the little n—— gal?" she asked.

Carol and I froze. We had been taught to never use that word. We knew the word had weight to it, that it was like a bludgeon, that it was mean, and hateful, and that if you ever said it, it meant there was something wrong with you. We never expected Miss Sweet or Miss Lovey to say something like that, and we didn't know what to do.

Baby knew. "I'm Baby," she said. "I'm Rosa's girl, Rosa that helps Miss Tennie."

"Well, what in the Sam Hill are you doing in my backyard?" Miss Pet asked.

"We're going to the library," Carol said.

"There's a sidewalk in the front of the house," Sweet said. "Wouldn't that be easier? Carolyn Mitchell ain't going to let the little n—— in the library anyway."

"Baby and I are going to wait while Judy goes in and gets some books. We're not going in," Carol said.

Miss Sweet clapped her hands. "Well, you and Baby can stay here with us then, and keep us company, can't you?"

Miss Lovey was busy pulling some rusted metal lawn chairs toward a shady spot in the corner of the yard where the bowl of an ancient birdbath was propped in the bed of a broken wheelbarrow. "This is my favorite spot!" Then she turned her attention to Baby. "Do you know that my name is Lovey, and my sister here is named Sweet? And I bet if my mama had had another child, she'd have named her Baby, like you!" The two sisters laughed.

Baby smiled politely and nodded at them. "I'm glad to meet you, Miss Lovey, and you too, Miss Sweet."

Lovey and Sweet looked like they were settling in for the whole afternoon. "I'm going on to the library," I said. "We've got to take care of our business and get home." I thought that sounded important.

I made the fastest trip to the library I'd ever made, scooping up five new books, the limit, and headed back through the privet hedge to Lovey and Sweet's. When I got back, the women and Carol were sitting in the metal chairs with glasses of iced tea, and Baby was standing up behind Carol with a mason jar of water. Carol was finishing up telling some story about her little brothers getting into the blackberry wine that Aunt Ethelle kept under the kitchen sink to pour on the Christmas fruitcake. Lovey and Sweet slapped their fat thighs and laughed. Then Miss Lovey looked up at Baby. "Tell us what you folks do on Saturday night. We heard y'all like to dance and sing and have a big time out there in Phillipsburg on Saturday night."

"We've got to leave now," I interrupted, but Lovey and Sweet didn't want to let us go.

"You come sit down," Lovey said. "I'll get you some tea. I've got some cookies. We can have a tea party."

I was worried about Mama and Rosa finding out we were gone, but I didn't want to upset the Davis sisters. It would be even worse for us if they decided we were being rude. They'd let Mama know about it for sure. I wondered what Mama would do to get away in this situation, and it came to me. "We sure wish we could stay all day," I said. "But you know Mama has that bad heart. She'd be so worried about us and we're supposed to do all we can to keep her calm."

There was nothing the Davis sisters could say to that, so off we went. We got back in time to sit ourselves at the picnic table and start to sort out the books before Rosa came out carrying a plate full of peanut butter and jelly sandwiches and bananas and a pitcher of sweet iced tea for our lunch. Rosa went back in the house while we ate.

We munched quietly for a while, swatting the gnats away when they bothered us. Then Carol put down her banana and said, "Miss Lovey and Miss Sweet are cuckoo!"

"They are crazy and cuckoo!" I added, and put my sandwich on my plate.

Baby kept eating, not looking us in the eye. Carol and I were staring at her, so finally she said, "Like most white folks."

I could read Carol's mind. We both wanted so badly for Baby to say, "But not you! And not Miss Tennie! Not Mr. Elwyn!" that we almost fainted from not breathing, but she didn't say anything more.

It wasn't much later on in the afternoon that Mama called us to come in and try the peach jam. She and Rosa were finished with their work. She split open some cold biscuits, toasted them with butter, and put a bowl full of the jam, still warm, on the table with the biscuits. She and Rosa joined us three girls and we ate and ate and thought nothing ever tasted so good.

Mama paid Rosa and packed some jars of beans and tomatoes and peach jam in a cardboard box for her to bring with her when my daddy came to drive her and Baby home. I thought we were safe. I thought our trip to the library would stay a secret between Carol and me. I figured we would have to chew on it for a long time, but that it would just be between us.

A week later, I was at Mama's and sat down in one of the rockers on the porch next to her while she was crocheting some pink baby booties. She didn't look at me, just kept on with her work. "I saw Miss Lovey and Miss Sweet the other day," she said. "They told me you and Carol and Baby were in their backyard last week."

"Uh-huh," I said. There wasn't much point in saying anything else.

"Actually, what they said was y'all were there with 'a little n——gal,'" she continued.

I rocked harder.

"Do you know why I told you girls to stay in the backyard?"

"No, ma'am," I said.

"That's why," Mama said.

"Oh." I looked over at Mama. She had a hard and sad look in her eyes.

"I don't tell you girls things just to hear the sound of my own voice. I told you for a reason to stay in the back, and you didn't do it. Just so you know, I talked with your cousin yesterday."

"We didn't think—" I started. I wanted to say we didn't think it would hurt anything to do what we did, but Mama stopped me.

"You didn't think, and that's the problem. How'd you like it if two old white ladies called you a 'n——'?"

My eyes started to burn with tears. "I don't guess I'd like it," I said in a whisper because I was so ashamed.

"There's a lot of meanness in this world that you don't even know about, and you and Carol put that child in a place where she had to be smacked in the face with some of it. An eight-year-old child! I thought the two of you were her friends!"

That may have been the angriest I ever saw Mama. She got up and left me on the porch, like she couldn't bear to sit with me. After a while, I got on my bike and rode home. Baby's face kept coming up in front of me, and I wished with all my heart that we had stayed in Mama's backyard.

Carol and I kept our distance from Rosa for some time. Around Halloween, she was cleaning at Carol's house, and I took the chance that she had cooled down and asked her how Baby was. She said Addie

Mae had made plans to bring Baby to Chicago with her after Christmas, that the schools were good there, and she'd have a better chance. I was glad to hear it. I hoped that in Chicago Baby would have a library she could go to anytime she wanted, and that the only thing the librarian checked when she went in was whether or not her hands were clean, that it wouldn't matter if she was black or white.

***

The next time we saw Baby was when Mama died. It was right after Christmas 1960. Carol, Baby, and I had graduated from high school in June of that year, Carol and I from Tifton High, and Baby from a school in Chicago. We all had a few months of college under our belts then. Baby was in town because she had come to visit Rosa for the holidays, and Rosa asked her to drive her to the funeral. She looked like a picture out of a magazine in her Chicago clothes. She and Rosa sat at the back of the funeral parlor all by themselves where black people sat when they came to white people's funerals. When it was over and people were milling around, Carol and I went over to talk to Baby, but none of us had much to say, broken up as we were about Mama, even though she'd been telling us she was dying for the last ten years and had had a pink lace dress made to be buried in last year. We should have been ready for it to happen.

Daddy got Rosa to have Baby bring her over to the house for some refreshments after the burial, but after they got there, Rosa wouldn't sit down in the living room with the rest of us. She kept asking if we needed any help in the kitchen, and when Aunt Ethelle insisted she wasn't there to work but to visit, she and Baby didn't stay long. After they left, I kept thinking of things I wished we could have talked about with Baby, and I wished that I could have told her I was sorry about that time with the library and Sweet and Lovey. But I knew there was no way those conversations were ever going to happen.

We never saw Baby again after Mama's funeral. We didn't see Rosa again either. I believe in my heart that Baby made something of herself in Chicago, but I don't have any real information about her.

Billy McGraw

FALL 1951

If the Wingos hadn't decided to take Billy McGraw on trial adoption from the Methodist Home for Boys the same year my daddy left and I quit talking, things might have worked out better for him. I don't know.

It was fourth grade, and we should have still been at Annie Belle Clark Elementary School. All the classes before us got to stay there until they finished fifth grade before being pushed up to the junior high school, but big work was planned for ABC, and they wanted us out of the way.

Schoolhouse fires in Atlanta and Milledgeville had been in the news the year before, and some people in town were sure we were next, that a fierce blaze would come and burn us up in that old tinderbox where our parents and some of our grandparents had also gone to school. There wasn't any money for a new building, so the school superintendent got the idea to put fire escapes in the old one. The top two floors of ABC, where the fourth and fifth grades usually had their classrooms, would be closed for the year, and we'd be sent on over to the junior high. The junior high didn't have space for us, so they got little portables, like house trailers, and sprinkled them around the junior high grounds among the azaleas and pine trees.

Annie Belle Clark might have been a tinder box, but it was stately and solid. Climbing the ten wide marble steps to the tall double doors made you feel like you were important. Climbing the three shaky wooden steps into the portable was like going into a shed. I felt like we'd been demoted, like the town didn't care about us anymore. The first day I went to the junior high campus and my mother led me to my assigned portable, I wondered what good could possibly come out of that flimsy little room. On top of that, our teacher, Mrs. Hill, left after a month, and we went through one substitute teacher after another. And on top of even that, Carol and her family moved away to Ocilla where her daddy had gotten a better job.

It was right then, in October, that my daddy left, and the rest of my world came apart. He'd been gone a lot in the weeks before, and for a while, my mother gave us reasons why. He'd gone to North Georgia to visit a cousin, or he had some training he had to take with the post office up in Macon. But then one day, she said he was coming home but he wouldn't be staying, and he had something to tell Lowell and me. I didn't get it, why he'd be telling her to tell us he had something to tell us. Why didn't he just tell us?

So, when he came, my mother left the house and my daddy said for us to sit down in the living room. Lowell sat in the blue stuffed chair that went with the sofa. He looked little and scared in that big chair. He was twelve, with buckteeth. He hadn't gotten his braces yet. I felt sorry for him and wanted to hold his hand, but I knew he wouldn't let me. I sat on the edge of the sofa and waited, but I was excited more than scared because it was such a strange thing to be doing, and I was so happy to have my daddy home.

He sat on the sofa with me and, after he coughed and cleared his throat a few times, he said, "I need to let you two know that I'm not going to be living with you kids and your mother anymore. I'll still come to see you, and when I get a place where you can come, you can spend time with me at my place, but I'm not going to be here."

"Can I come with you?" I asked him.

"No," he said. "Not now." He put his arms around me. "I'll come see you when I can." Then he told Lowell, "You're going to have to be the man of the house since I'm leaving."

Lowell looked even smaller and more scared, but he just nodded, so I nodded too. I didn't say anything else, not then, and not until sometime in the spring. It wasn't that I made up my mind not to talk or thought about it. It was that my daddy leaving was too horrible a thing to believe, and I knew that if I did not put any words to it, it wouldn't be true. So I didn't. I went inside myself and watched as life went on around me, like watching a movie, but a movie that you were acting in yourself. Or it was like being in a dream where you see everything happening in the dream and you're dreaming it too.

I watched my mother cry. I watched while she got angry when I didn't answer her. I watched while she said awful things about my daddy to her sisters. I watched Lowell get more worried and scared. I watched my teacher, a new one every few weeks, write on the board and give us lessons. I did what my mother and my teachers told me to do, but not a word came out of my mouth. A single word would have made it all real. I knew I was going to die the minute it became real.

Christmas came and I wrote in my letter to Santa Claus that the only thing I wanted was for Daddy to come home, which was to admit he was gone. It was OK for me to write the words as long as I didn't say them. On Christmas Day, Mother, Lowell, and I opened our presents in the morning, and Daddy came in the afternoon and took Lowell and me to Mama and Papa's house for Christmas dinner. I watched all of them laugh and say "Merry Christmas" and hug one another, and I smelled the Christmas tree and the turkey, and ate the chocolate candy, but didn't say a word. My letter to Santa Claus didn't work. After Daddy took us home, he drove away again.

After Christmas, life went on like before. I don't know how many weeks went by, but it was beginning to get warmer, and at school, at recess, I'd go off by myself, weaving pine-straw bracelets or climbing on the monkey bars, which were at the far edge of the area we fourth graders were supposed to use. I had just learned how to "walk," hanging by my hands all the way across the monkey bars from one end to the other, when Billy McGraw joined our class.

***

After I quit talking, my mother often took me with her to visit her friends. As soon as the subject of my silence came up, she'd explain that it happened after my daddy left. One day, we were at Pastor Wingo's house visiting his wife. She told us that she had been to a program about the Methodist Home for Boys in Albany and was thinking about taking in a boy. The Wingos' son was grown and in college, and she was lonely. My mother remarked that she had the preacher for company. Mrs. Wingo said, "You'd think so, but it's like being alone. Pastor Wingo gives more attention to his flock than he does to me."

My mother looked embarrassed and just said, "Well, I see," in a halting kind of way. Maybe she was thinking about the fact that we were part of Pastor Wingo's flock and took up some of his time.

A few weeks later, Billy McGraw showed up in my class. Our teacher, Miss Lassiter, told us that he was the Wingo's new boy. He was short and chunky with a fleshy face and big lips that hung open. He didn't smile. He just kept looking around behind his back like he was expecting somebody to sneak up on him. It made me think the other boys at the Methodist Home must have been a sorry lot if Billy McGraw was the best the Wingos could do in picking out one to bring home. I wondered how he liked it at the Wingos' house with all the crocheted doilies on the chair backs.

It was maybe a couple of weeks after Billy came that I was playing on the monkey bars at recess one afternoon. All the other kids were a little way apart from where I was, jumping rope or swinging or chasing each other and falling on the ground. They seemed to understand about me, that I needed to be left alone, like I had a handicap or something.

I was still working on getting from one end of the monkey bars to the other in a graceful way, swinging side to side, slapping my hands alternately onto one bar and then the next one and the next. When I'd first learned the trick, I was awkward, without the rhythm of it. But now I pretty much had it down and thought maybe I'd be good enough to be in the circus if I kept at it. I was wrapped in my own world thinking about the acrobats I'd seen one time in the circus when I heard Billy McGraw yell, "Git out of my way!" and saw him hanging by his arms at the other end of the bars. His red plaid shirt had come untucked, and his pants had slipped down around his hips to where his underwear showed. His navel stuck out like a pinched up mouth in the middle of his fat belly and he was lunging along, making his way toward my end of the bars. His face was puffy and red, and he snorted and panted with the effort. "I said back up, you dummy! Git out of my way."

I didn't know what to do. I'd have backed up if I'd known how, but I didn't. I'd tried a few times, but going backward is different from going forward. You have to reach back and feel for the bar behind you and then grab on to it tight enough to support yourself and to trust to let go of the bar in front. I'd planned to learn that next, but so far, hadn't learned how, so I just hung there while Billy McGraw flailed and screamed. He pulled his legs up to kick at me, but instead, he fell off the bars onto the hard ground on his knees.

The way I was then, I watched from inside myself while Billy got up with his bleeding knees and his red angry face and ran at me, with me still hanging from the bars. He wrapped his arms around my legs and yanked until I fell splat on my back. It knocked the air out of me. I tried to sit up, but Billy McGraw pushed me down and sat on my chest. He kept yelling, calling me dummy. Then he started hitting me in the face with his fists.

I knew that somehow it wasn't fair to Billy for me to be like I was. He could hit me all day long, and it wouldn't matter to me. To him, I was a normal girl with feelings and fears lying on the ground under him while he was pounding at me, but to myself, I was just watching all this happen like he was beating up a rag doll. I didn't feel it. And it was making him madder and madder.

I heard Sonny Parkman yell, "Get Mr. Jackson!" Right after that, Mr. Corky Jackson, who was the principal and who had been a prisoner of war in Japan and could handle anything, came at a trot, smiling and calm, his suit coat flapping out behind him, and lifted Billy McGraw off me like he was picking up a kitten.

Mrs. Green, who worked in Mr. Jackson's office, was right behind him, gathering me up in her arms, smoothing down my skirt, wiping my mouth with a handkerchief. She led me into the schoolhouse, the main building, and into the teachers' lounge which was so full of cigarette smoke that I coughed and blood sprayed all over her white blouse. I felt bad about that. Some of the teachers came over to look at me: "Take her to the doctor," "Call her mother," and mumbling about "that boy from the Methodist home...no place for that here in this school...It's not right."

Mrs. Paulk, who was Julia Paulk's mother and Dr. Peatman's nurse, brought me and Mrs. Green in from the waiting room as soon as we arrived at his office. She had a look on her face that made me wonder just how hurt I was. She took off my dress, which was embarrassing to me, standing there in my slip in front of Mrs. Green. I wished I'd worn my nice nylon slip instead of the old cotton one I had on.

By the time Mother arrived, both my eyes were puffed and closing so that I could only see through little slits. "What in the world?" she asked. "How did you get into a fight?" She looked worried and reached out to lay her hand on my cheek. Mrs. Green told her I had not gotten into a fight, that Billy McGraw had jumped on me, that it wasn't my fault. She left and went back to school.

Dr. Peatman put a couple of stitches over my right eye. He told me I'd be fine. Then he swiveled around to my mother on his stool. "When did she quit talking?" My mother began to cry, and started telling him about my daddy leaving. Dr. Peatman called Mrs. Paulk and asked her to take me out of the room.

That afternoon, my daddy came to the house. He took me in his arms like a baby and finally I was safe enough to cry. For the first time since he left, my mother didn't leave the house while Daddy was there. She stood by the kitchen door and told him that Dr. Peatman said I was hysterical, which confused me. I'd been to movies where women were called hysterical when they were screaming and wild, and I wasn't anything like that.

Daddy came by the next day and the day after that. Mother kept staying around, and they talked a little bit and seemed friendlier. Then one morning after a couple of weeks, Daddy was there when we woke up, and we knew he had stayed all night.

Billy McGraw got suspended from school for a week after he beat me up. When he came back, they put him in a different classroom to see if that would help, but it didn't. The teacher caught him smoking a cigarette behind the portable, and he called her an old bitch, which got him suspended again. Then he hit Tommy Waldrop during PE with a baseball, on purpose, and broke his tooth.

The Wingos were trying to figure out what to do about Billy when Sheriff Anderson picked him up five miles out on Highway 41, trying to make his way back to the Methodist Home. That helped the Wingos decide they couldn't handle him, and they agreed to return him to people who might be able to deal with him better than they could. On their drive back from Albany, they saw a sign on a farmhouse lawn advertising Border collie puppies and bought a beautiful ten-week-old tricolor female Mrs. Wingo called Maggie, who did more to relieve her loneliness than Billy McGraw ever had a hope of doing.

I came back into myself and began to talk again. We never spoke about it. I was just not talking one day, and I was talking the next. It was the same way we didn't speak about my daddy leaving and coming back. Even though he was back, we rarely felt like a family after that. If Daddy could leave one time, he could leave another time, and we were all waiting for that next time. The ground under our feet had gone shaky. Life continued on that new shaky foundation. Still, his being present let me have enough of a grip on life to speak.

Lowell didn't have much to do with Daddy after he came back. He started spending more time with his friends and their families and less with us. Whatever you want to say about Tifton, the town provided us with what we needed. Love and kindness are love and kindness, no matter where they come from. There were plenty of adults of good intent who were ready to fill in the gaps our own parents left, and parents always do leave gaps. No one daddy or one mother can provide everything.

For a long time, I wondered about how it would have been back then for Billy McGraw if I had been a talking person when he told me to get off the bars. If, when he yelled at me to go back, I'd said, "I'd be glad to go back if I could, but I don't know how," maybe then he'd have said OK and waited for his turn. Then I'd have shown him about the rhythm for walking on your hands across the bars, and we'd have made friends, and he'd not have smoked a cigarette or hit Tommy Waldrop with the baseball. Knowing how one thing builds on another and we go down the path that's laid out that way, I just wondered.

***

When we were juniors in high school, Billy McGraw showed up again. I don't know who he was living with at that point, but it wasn't the Wingos because Pastor Wingo had retired and they had moved away. Every once in a while, I'd get a glimpse of Billy in the hallways after he came back, but we never spoke, never had a class together, and never even caught each other's eye. It was like that whole thing with him beating me up had not ever happened, but when I'd see him, my heart always stopped for a split second while I remembered how he looked at me that day.

After high school, I didn't give much thought to him again until we went to Tifton to attend the reunion for the thirtieth, and I saw his picture blown up on a billboard out on the interstate, advertising his barbecue place. "Billy McGraw's, Best Ribs in the South," it said in big red letters. Billy was grinning in the picture and wearing a straw hat and checkered shirt and overalls, like a country bumpkin, in a way that probably appealed to the Yankees driving on I-75 on their way to Florida. Billy provided barbecue for the reunion picnic that year as well as for the fortieth and the fiftieth reunions. He always looked happy and successful, standing over the big drum grill, wielding a barbecue fork and spatula, moving ribs this way and that over the fire. We'd smile at each other, but not a word ever passed between us while I stood in the buffet line and held out my plate for him to pile it up with barbecue.

Nasty Ray
FALL 1952

It took me from Friday until Monday, which is a very long time, to get up the courage to tell Mother the whole thing about Nasty Ray and Gladys and the puppy, because I knew she'd be angry. But I had to tell her if I was going to have a chance. It was the most important thing in the world. It wasn't like I wanted the puppy. I *needed* it. Finally, after I searched through my mind for the best way to go about it and couldn't come up with anything that would for sure make her say yes, I just went on and told her.

It was in the middle of September, only a week before my birthday, which I hoped would help, because she might be feeling more kindly toward me right then. I had just walked in from school and went into the kitchen where she was standing in front of the stove with her blue, polka-dot apron on. She was stirring spaghetti sauce, which smelled like heaven. I hoped the cozy smell might warm her up to what I had to tell her.

"That's going to be yummy," I said. Then I launched right into it. "I've been talking to Nasty Ray," I went on, like it were nothing at all, something I might do any day of the week, and thought she would be interested in.

She turned around and looked at me, and her mouth dropped open. "What do you mean?" She asked, like she couldn't understand what I'd said.

"Only out in his front yard," I said. "I didn't go near the house or anything."

"You shouldn't have even been on his side of the street!" she said.

"Oh," I said, and looked down at my feet. "I know I'm not supposed to walk on the sidewalk by the pool hall, but I don't remember you telling me not to walk in front of Nasty Ray's." I was lying, because I did know, and she knew I knew, but I took the chance that she'd be too tired of dealing with me to have a fit about it.

She must have been, because she just shook her head and looked sort of disgusted. "Did he hurt you or anything? Did he try to put his hands on you?"

"No, ma'am," I said. "He's real nice. He…" I tried to think about how to finish saying what I needed to say, but I couldn't come up with a roundabout way, and went on and blurted it out. "Gladys is going to have puppies, and he said maybe I could have one."

Mother looked at me like I had suddenly turned into a frog, like she was so shocked she couldn't get words to come out of her mouth. I took advantage of the situation to plow ahead and acted like I didn't see how upset she was.

"He didn't promise me. He said we could maybe take one of them and let her see if she likes us, and if Gladys feels OK about it. That's after the puppies get to be two months old, so it's a long time off. The puppies won't even be born for another couple of weeks."

"You can't have a dog!" Mother said. "I have told you until I'm blue in the face."

"I'll take care of it," I said. "It won't be any trouble to you or to Daddy," I said. "Do you know which one is Gladys?"

"I don't care which one she is!" Mother said. "How many dogs does he have, anyway? Ten? Fifteen? All chasing behind him on one of those bicycles all over town like a pack of wolves. Mongrels, every one of them." She shook her head and went back to stirring the spaghetti sauce.

Even with what she said, on my part, I felt hopeful. The puppies weren't born yet, so there was still time. At least I'd told her, and so she had to be thinking about it.

When Daddy came home from work, I was practicing hopscotch on the concrete slab at the bottom of the steps in the backyard. The kitchen window was open, and I overheard Mother and him talking and her telling him about me and Nasty Ray, and me asking for a puppy. In the past, when I'd asked, he'd said no just like she had, but I hoped this time was going to be different. After all, this time it was a real puppy I was asking for, one I knew where to get, not just an idea of a dog.

Daddy came outside and sat on the steps. "Your mother said you've been visiting with Nasty Ray."

I explained it all to him and he nodded his head and said, "I see." Then he said, "The fire department condemned Nasty Ray's house again last week. This makes about five times he's been condemned. Place is a fire hazard. All those dogs. Health department wants it cleaned up, too, or torn down. No one should be living in those conditions."

I was encouraged that he hadn't mentioned the puppy. It seemed like the main problem was Nasty Ray's house, not me having a dog.

The thing about Nasty Ray was that he didn't carry on his life like other people, but he lived on a street where regular people lived. In fact, he lived on Love Avenue four blocks from downtown right between the Stevensons and the McKays, who kept their yards up nice with azaleas and camellias, and dogwood and redbud trees blooming in the spring, and rows of boxwoods along the walkways, so that when you went by, you had to look at them and admire how beautiful they were. Then in the middle of them was Nasty Ray's house with nothing but bare dirt in the yard and blackberry vines growing over the front porch so that the only way to get into the house was through the back door, and pieces of broken down bicycles strewn around, and who knows how many dogs lying in piles sleeping or digging holes in the yard.

Nasty Ray had always lived there so far as I knew. When people said "Nasty Ray," it was just like it was the name his mama and daddy had given him, and I don't believe anyone even thought about it being rude to call him that. It was simply his name, but they didn't call him that to his face. They called him Ray to his face.

Papa Ireland said he had known Ray when he was growing up although he was a few years older than Ray. Papa said Ray's parents had been nice, normal people, and Ray was their only child. He said Ray was a "different" kind of boy, but not so odd that he couldn't find a girl to marry him when he was a young man. She was from Adele, and her family had made some money from an insurance business, and her daddy set Ray up to work for him selling insurance. The girl died after a few years, and Ray quit the insurance work and came back to Tifton to live with his parents and work at repairing bicycles. He seemed a little "off," but generally OK. Then when his parents died, he started letting everything go and accumulating dogs, and people started calling him "Nasty Ray."

A lot of people didn't like that Ray's house looked so bad and tried to get the sheriff to step in and find some way to get him out of there, but every time the house got condemned, he'd do what he had to do to pass inspection, and then let it go again until the next time it got condemned.

The other thing, besides his house, that Ray did to call attention to himself was to ride one of his bicycles through town streaming dogs behind him like he was a comet with a fiery tail, not of stars but of dogs running and barking behind him. Sometimes the tail of dogs was half a block long, every dog different from the next, and for me, it was a wonder. I wanted a dog so bad it almost broke my heart to see Nasty Ray with that vast wealth of them, and me not allowed to have even one little puppy.

Despite Mother's warning not to go past Nasty Ray's house, I'd been walking by there for weeks before all this happened. I walked all over town anyway. I could go wherever I wanted as long as I got home before dark. Of course, there was the rule about going by the pool hall. I followed that rule because it made sense to me with all the smoke pouring out the door every time it was opened, and men going in and coming out. I didn't have any interest in being there anyway. Nasty Ray's was another matter. I was drawn to the dogs like a bee to a bunch of wisteria.

At first, I only stood on the sidewalk in front of his house and looked at them. After a while, one of them started coming up to me and asking me to scratch behind her ears. She was the prettiest one, I thought, and the smartest. She looked a bit like Lassie but not exactly. Her fur was shorter than Lassie's, but she was that color. And she remembered me from one time to another. I started bringing her pieces of bacon from my breakfast or a little corner of my sandwich from lunch. It got to where she would see me from down the street and run up to me.

Then one day when I went by, Ray was working on a bicycle he had hanging upside down on a stand in his front yard. When she ran over to me, he called out that her name was Gladys and that she was going to have puppies soon. He watched us for a while, and when he saw how we got along, he said, "She likes you." That made me really happy.

It was a few days after that that I asked him how much the puppies would cost when they got here. "I don't sell no dogs," he said, like the question had offended him. "Only thing I do is, if there is somebody special who I think would give one of them a good home, and if the mother likes the person, and if the puppy likes the person, I may let them adopt one after the puppy gets to be two months old. That's a lot of ifs."

He looked me up and down. "You're an Ireland, aren't you? Which one is your daddy?" I told him, and he nodded. "You thinking about applying for one of Gladys' puppies?"

"Yes, but I have to ask my parents."

He said he'd take it "under advisement."

***

Daddy listened. "One of Nasty Ray's puppies," he said and smiled. "That's the very last place I ever figured on getting a dog." He said he'd talk to Mother and to Ray, and that he'd think about it. "I didn't say yes, now," he said. "Don't go believing you're getting this puppy. I only said I'd give it some thought."

He made me repeat what he'd said, that he had not promised me the puppy. Well, that was all it took for me to feel like it was Christmas morning. I jumped up and hugged him. It helped with Mother that Lowell said he also wanted a dog. Daddy had come around to the idea of it by then, so it was three against one. She gave in.

We thought that was the end of it, that as soon as the puppies made their entrance, we'd start a two-month countdown and then we'd have our puppy. Carol and her sister, Jo, came over for my birthday, along with some other kids. We had cake and ice cream and played games, and I opened presents, but the main thing I wanted to do was to tell everybody about the puppy. When I said we were getting it from Nasty Ray, every single one of them asked why and turned up their noses like something smelled bad. I didn't care.

I was trying hard to be as good as I could be at home so Mother wouldn't change her mind. I didn't talk back, which was the thing I did that made her the maddest. I made my bed. I set the table. I did everything she asked me to do. And I didn't go by Nasty Ray's, like she said.

So I hadn't seen him or Gladys for a couple of weeks when Daddy went over to talk with him. He hadn't told me he was going that day. He just came in from work late and told us.

"I paid a visit to Ray today," he said. "Interesting fellow. Busy cleaning up his yard for the fire department's inspection. Told him about us wanting one of the puppies, which came last night, by the way."

I got excited at this news. "Can I go see them?"

"Well, you can go see them if it's OK with your mother," Daddy said. "But he hasn't decided yet if we can have one. I had to fill out some papers about us for him."

"Why wouldn't he let us have one?" Mother asked.

"He said he has to meet you and Lowell before he decides if we'd be acceptable. He's OK with me and Judy because he knows us."

Mother said, "I'm not going over there to that mess! There're probably rats all over the place. He ought to be happy we'd be willing to take one of his mongrel dogs. Here he's acting like we're not fit to have a puppy!" She was really mad.

Daddy asked Mother if she would rather invite Ray to our house to let him meet her here instead of at his house.

"And have him ride his bicycle down 14th Street with ten dogs tearing behind him? I would not!"

Daddy said that was not the right language to use if we were going to convince Ray to let us have a puppy.

So eventually she took Lowell and visited Ray, and I guess they passed his test because when they came home, they said the next thing we needed to do was pick out which puppy we wanted.

Lowell and I went to make our choice when the puppies were six weeks old. It may have been the last time we ever did anything together like that. And it felt as if our parents were in it with us (even though Mother had had to be persuaded), like we were a family rather than the way things usually were then, with all of us off in different directions. Ray took us around to his back porch, where Gladys lay in a big square box padded with a bunch of towels, seven of the cutest and sweetest creatures I'd ever imagined crawling all over her. We picked them up one at a time, them squirming and licking, and neither Lowell nor I could quit grinning. I had never smelled a puppy, and when I did, I knew nothing had ever smelled that good before. I wanted to bring every one of them home to love on them all day and night.

It was hard to choose just one, but finally we settled on a little girl whose tail ended in a white tip, and named her Tippie. Ray got out the papers that Daddy had filled out on us and wrote down that Tippie was ours if the home visits worked out. Then we waited two more weeks before we could take her for an afternoon. She seemed to like our house and ran all around with us. I tied some old socks into a ball, like Ray told me to do, and she chewed and pulled at it, and seemed to be happy. When we took her back that day, Ray still didn't say definitely we could have her. I almost gave up hope right then because I didn't know what we had done wrong, and how could I fix it if I didn't know what it was?

But, a day later, Daddy went by Ray's, and Ray said we could take Tippie for an overnight visit. By then, she was two months old, and it was getting close to Christmas. The overnight went well, at least as far as Ray knew. We didn't tell him about Tippie wetting the floor in the kitchen, and Mother threatening to never let her in the house again because when she was growing up, dogs stayed in the yard and that was where they belonged. She didn't keep her threat. She was in love with Tippie, too, by then. We all were. Ray wrote out a paper that said that Tippie was ours and made us say we'd bring her back over from time to time to see him and her mother, which we did. She was finally ours, and all I wanted to do was hold her and kiss her. And when I put her down, Lowell was right there throwing a stick for her to learn to bring back, and when he got tired of that, Mother was squatting down to pet her and talk baby talk to her. Daddy just smiled and watched and looked pleased.

We had a good Christmas. Tippie helped a lot, like she was a new baby, and we were in a real family. I had to think about Baby Jesus and how happy he must have made everybody when he was born, just like Tippie made us. I didn't tell anybody about that, though. They probably wouldn't have understood about Jesus being like a puppy.

While Ray was so careful about us as pet owners, he didn't think to worry about our neighbors. None of us did. We should have.

Louise Shepherd and her husband lived next door. They were scientists at the Coastal Plain Experiment Station out on the edge of town. They had come to Tifton from somewhere else and were not interested in being friendly. They had no children and had made it clear that they didn't like children even a little bit. If Lowell or I stepped one foot into their front yard, and if they were home, one of them came out and said how we were tearing up their grass. We stayed away from them. "They are sad people," Daddy had said. "Don't be bothered about them. You just stay off their grass." Well, we did, but Tippie couldn't figure out what the difference was between our lawn and the Shepherds' so they yelled at us a lot after Tippie came.

Our time with sweet Tippie was sadly short. Lowell and I were at school when Mother found her in our side yard under the willow tree, passed away and already stiff. When we got home, she was sitting in the living room with Tippie's dead body wrapped in a towel in her lap, crying and stroking her and saying how sorry she was. I didn't know I could hurt so bad until that day. When Daddy had left, I'd gone numb and didn't feel much. This time, the pain came in and took over, and I could feel every bit of it. I didn't think I'd ever be happy again. Daddy came home from work and took Tippie's body to the veterinarian, to try to find out what happened to her. She had not been sick; there was no reason for her to die. It didn't make any sense. He may have had a suspicion about the Shepherds, but I don't know. The vet confirmed that she had been given poisoned meat. He knew that the scientists at the experiment station worked with poisons but didn't know what kind, or what kind had killed Tippie, and couldn't prove anything. We all concluded, right or wrong, that Louise Shepherd had done it.

Daddy dug a grave for Tippie under the tree where Mother had found her. We were all too stunned to say much when we buried her. We just cried. Daddy and I went to see Ray, who had cleaned his house enough to get released from the condemnation order. We said Tippie had been poisoned but not about our suspicions of the Shepherds because Daddy didn't trust what Ray might do. Ray just kept telling us not to blame ourselves, that there were some terrible people in the world.

The worst thing that happened after Tippie got killed was when I told Mother that at least Tippie was now in heaven with Jesus. It had consoled me to think about her running around Jesus' feet, jumping up on Him, tugging at His robes, having a good time, Jesus reaching down to pet her. I hung on to that picture. But Mother looked at me straight in the eye and said that dogs don't go to heaven. I argued with her, but she said she knew this for a fact. It took me a while, but I realized at some point that she didn't know any more than I did about where dogs go when they die, and that a belief that didn't allow for dogs to be in heaven was not one I could accept. I could come up with my own beliefs.

Dogs go to heaven and that's the truth. I know it for a fact.

***

Ray lived in his house on Love Avenue along with his dogs for a few more years. I didn't go back to see him, or them, again. It made me too sad. Sometime when I was in high school, driving by his house with one of my friends, I noticed that the house looked vacant and asked Daddy about it. He said Ray had sold his place and moved to the country, and he had taken all the dogs with him. He'd heard that Ray was happy out there, and that the dogs had lots of room to run around, and he could make as much mess as he wanted without bothering anybody else.

Tippie will live forever, with all her sweet puppiness, as the answer to the security question, "What was the name of your first pet?" I type in "Tippie" and smile and remember her. The name "Louise Shepherd," likewise, will forever be synonymous with the name of the devil herself.

Marlene and Darlene

WINTER 1952

The twins tapped and hopped and leaped into the air, and came down in perfect, synchronized splits. They shuffled and twirled little top hats on brass-capped canes along to their mother's cheerful piano while she smiled wide at them and kept a steady beat with her chin. From kindergarten on, the twins danced like they had been born into the world wearing sequined costumes and tiny tap shoes. If there was a stage, they were on it, and there were lots of stages. There were dance recitals, and school assembly programs, and parades where they danced on flatbed trucks going down the middle of Main Street. And all the time, while they were kicking up their heels and swinging their arms, they grinned like they were having the most fun anybody could ever have. Maybe most remarkable, they were able to do this and not be show-offy about it, like all they wanted was to make us happy.

Marlene and Darlene were identical, down to the moles on their left cheeks. The only way to tell them apart was that Darlene was a bit quieter. She usually let Marlene take the lead. If you asked the two of them a question, Marlene answered first. And, while Marlene always wore a grin like she were constantly in the middle of a frenetic dance routine, Darlene often carried a more thoughtful look. Mrs. Dunbarton dressed them in matching clothes, onstage and off, including even their socks and underwear. I know this because I asked one time, and Marlene obligingly lifted her skirt, then Darlene's, to show me the pink-flowered panties they both had on.

The twins were my age. I admired them so much that when I was six, I wheedled my mother into signing me up for dance lessons with them at Betty Jean Clemons' School of Dance. However, after my third lesson, my career was cut short when Betty Jean's husband piled all her clothes in the middle of their front yard and set a match to them. We missed the spectacle of the bonfire, but people who saw it said it was something to see, with the rhinestones on Betty Jean's costumes twinkling in the blaze, and the sequins melting into puddles on the grass. Marlene and Darlene resumed their classes after Betty Jean replaced her wardrobe, but I didn't. My mother decided that the whole episode was indicative of a flaw in Betty Jean's character that made her unfit to teach children. But if Betty Jean's character hurt Marlene and Darlene, I never saw any evidence of it.

Mr. Matt Herring was the owner of the Tift Theater. He had given us a peephole to look through into the world outside by bringing picture shows to town. We had always had the library, of course, the books, the words, but movies made it real. We got to see images of large cities, and mountains, and the West. We got to see Bible stories acted out, and big musicals with dancing and singing, and a lot more. The movies expanded our world. On the flip side, they also let us know just how insignificant we were, a minuscule gathering of souls living far less interesting and exciting lives than the ones on the screen.

Certainly, we were not as glamorous as the movie stars. We didn't talk in their snappy back and forth or dress in fancy clothes like they did. And we sure didn't have gunfights in the streets. However, there was one thing that we did have that proved that we were as good as the rest of the world. We had the Dunbarton twins. When we watched them tapping away up on a stage, we just knew that they were better than Fred Astaire and Ginger Rogers, or Gene Kelly, or any of the rest of them. We were sure that if they wanted to, the twins could go to Hollywood today and be on the silver screen tomorrow making millions of dollars and dazzling the world.

For a long time, Mr. Matt Herring had run a Saturday afternoon entertainment program for kids at the Tift Theater. He showed cartoons and a cowboy movie, followed by a serial. It was good for most of the afternoon. Then, when we were in fifth grade, he stepped up his program. I guess he didn't think he had absolutely every single kid in town sitting in the theater at noon on Saturday, so he threw in a talent show between the cartoons and the cowboy movie to bring in the few holdouts.

The talent show was a big success. All you had to do was come to the theater at eleven thirty and say what your talent was, and if you were among the first seven to sign up, you could be in the contest. The prizes changed from week to week. They included a ride in an airplane, which was a crop duster piloted by Mr. Herring's brother, or free movie tickets, popcorn and cokes, or a silver dollar. The prizes were OK, but it was really about the glory of the thing. Mr. Herring put the winner's name in big letters on a card in the corner of one of the movie posters outside the theater. It stayed there until the next Saturday, and everybody in town walking by saw it.

Kids performed in all kinds of ways. They sang, they recited Lee's "Farewell Address to the Army of Northern Virginia" and Joyce Kilmer's "Trees." They played piano and flute solos. One boy from out in the country did a hand jive, slapping his open palms on his thighs and chest and head, all the while making mouth noises to keep the rhythm. That was my favorite, next to the twins. Some kids danced. Of course, the twins danced.

After the performances, kids in the audience determined the winners by clapping, and whoever got the largest applause won. Actually, though, Mr. Herring made the final decision, since there wasn't any way to tell exactly the loudness of each round of applause. It wasn't hard to see that he used his own discretion to spread the winners around. The twins had won second place once, but never first. But then, they didn't enter the contest every week.

Carol and I couldn't figure out any talent that we had that was worth giving it a shot. I did have a knack for doing string figures, but when I tried to imagine standing up on the stage with outstretched arms and a loop of cord woven between my fingers, I knew it wouldn't work. If I had any doubt, Carol set me straight. "You'd just embarrass yourself," she said.

Instead, we settled on getting to the theater early to soak up the excitement of the performers. We'd arrive around eleven forty-five and sit on the right-hand side in the second row just behind the kids who had already signed up. They had to sit in the front row so they could go up on the stage when their time came. One Saturday when Marlene and Darlene were going to perform, they sat right in front of us.

"You're gonna come in first today," Carol leaned over and said to them. "It's time." I added my "Yeah. You're the best!"

Marlene and Darlene were wearing black and white costumes like miniature tuxedos with long tails and top hats. They glanced around, checking out the competition. Jane McMullins had signed up first, clutching her piano sheet music for "Moonlight Sonata." No problem there. Bobby Erwin sat beside Jane carrying a cloth bag of balls for his juggling act. He was good, but nothing like the twins. There were three or four other kids who recited or sang. That was it. It was almost 11:55 when a girl we didn't know ran down the middle aisle of the theater, all out of breath. She grabbed Mr. Herring's arm. "Me and my brother want to be in the show. I hope it's not too late. We came over from Sylvester."

Carol and I were about an arm's length away. We stayed quiet so we could hear what she was going to do.

"I'm Janice. He's Joey."

Mr. Herring said she was welcome, and where was Joey and what did they do?

She said, "He plays and I sing, and I'll go get him."

The next thing was that we saw the girl, who was about twelve, pushing a boy, a little younger, down the aisle in a wheelchair. The boy wore shorts, knobby knees sticking out, with braces on his legs. They looked somber. When they got to the first row where the contestants sat, Janice rolled Joey's chair up alongside the end of the folding seats. Jane got up and moved down so Janice could sit beside him. Neither of them looked at us. They just studied their sheet music. "Beautiful Dreamer," I noted.

Mr. Herring's custom was to draw the names of the contestants out of a hat to determine the order of the acts, so he wouldn't give anybody an advantage. It turned out that Janice and Joey were the next to the last act that day, and since Marlene and Darlene had not been called, they'd be last.

Mr. Herring, who wore a bow tie and suspenders for the performances, announced each of the acts in turn. When he got to the Willises, he said, "All the way from Sylvester"—it was twenty miles—"Janice and Joey Willis have come to give us a brother and sister act. Joey is the piano player, and Janice sings!"

Carol and I watched as Janice gathered Joey in her arms out of the wheelchair, just like she were picking up a doll, and carried him up the stairs onto the stage and set him down on the piano bench. None of us had ever seen a real disabled kid before. I don't know if any of us took a breath until Joey got his hands on the keys. The whole theater was quieter than church. Mr. Herring helped Janice get the microphone in position. But before she started singing, she said, "Joey had polio. That's why he can't walk."

The silence in the theater got even deeper. Polio. Polio hung over all of us, waiting to drop out of nowhere and kill, or maim, us. Our parents were terrified of it even more than we were. The mood in the room went from cheerful and boisterous before the Willises appeared to a stunned fear after the mention of polio.

Joey and Janice made it through "Beautiful Dreamer" OK. We clapped for them more out of relief that it was over than because of the performance.

After Mr. Herring announced Marlene and Darlene, Marlene set up their record player at the corner of the stage and put on "Darktown Strutters' Ball." It was weird from the beginning, with them coming on dancing right after Janice and Joey, and him being disabled. Then, when they got to the part about "I'm gonna dance off both my shoes," all anybody could think about was that little Joey was never, ever going to dance off even one of his shoes.

At the end, Mr. Herring always had the contestants line up, and he held his hand over them one at a time to have us clap again before he announced the winner. Janice stood in line with her arms around Joey's neck. He was back in his wheelchair by then. When Mr. Herring got to them, we all clapped hard. Marlene called out, "Janice and Joey!" Well, of course they won. We were glad, like maybe if they got the first prize, none of us would get polio. Anyway, they seemed happy.

After the show, Janice turned around and waved at the audience while she pushed Joey back up the aisle to the lobby. Their mother, who had been sitting in the rear with the few parents who came, stood up and smiled at us. We thought we had seen the last of them.

The Willises, however, did not let us off so lightly. They returned the very next week, smiling like homecoming heroes, carrying new sheet music. Those of us in Tifton knew that when you won first place, the polite thing to do was to hang back for a while to let someone else have a chance. I guess the Willises, being from Sylvester, didn't understand. It was embarrassing. You could tell that Mr. Herring didn't know quite what to do when Janice stood in front of him, asking him to sign them up again.

"We've got a new song," Janice said. "Flow Gently, Sweet Afton."

They had advanced from singing about a sleeping sweetheart to singing about a dead one. We all knew the songs because they were ones we sang in chorus at school.

"We've been working on it all week," Joey said.

Mr. Herring kept his voice low while he said to Janice, "OK, honey, but I need to tell you something. I'll let you be in the show today, since you came all the way over here, but you need to take a recess after that. When you win first place, you can't keep coming back week after week." Janice said OK.

The Willises still came in third, behind Leland Montgomery and his accordion and Felicity Campbell doing magic tricks. One more time, we figured the Willises had finished with the Tift Theater children's talent show.

It was several weeks later, the first time the twins returned to compete after losing to the Willises, that we were waiting with them for the show to start. They had on yellow rain slickers and were carrying yellow umbrellas. "Singin' in the Rain." I'd seen them do this routine a couple of times.

"I love this one!" I whispered to Marlene. "How do you move your feet so fast, so close, and not step on each other?"

"Just do!" Marlene grinned. She was looking back at the door from the lobby into the theater. Then I saw her face go in a second from smiling to something else, like worried or mad or surprised. I didn't even have to turn around to know what she was looking at. The Willises were back. Janice was pushing Joey down the aisle in a blue-checked dress with puffy sleeves and a white pinafore. She was way too old for a pinafore. They got signed up, and Janice sat down in her seat by Joey's wheelchair. "We're doing 'Sweet Little Buttercup,'" she whispered to me. Then she looked pointedly at Darlene. "I'm dancing," she said. "Sweet Little Buttercup" was a song for the smallest kids in dance recitals, not for big girls like Janice. We just said OK.

Mr. Herring pulled the Willises' name out for the third performance. I wished they had had a cousin like Carol who had said to them that if they did this act, they'd embarrass themselves. But they didn't. Janice looked so silly in that pinafore that you wanted to look away. Then, just like the first time they came, she told Mr. Herring she wanted to say something before they started.

"This is my first time dancing, and we want you all to know that we are praying to Jesus that all the boys and girls with polio will be able to dance someday. We hope you will pray with us."

The twins were now competing against a disabled kid and Jesus too. Well, after they performed there was a lot of applause, even though it was clear that Janice couldn't dance her way out of a paper bag.

The twins got called up after the Willises. Right before they got out of their seats, I saw Marlene turn and look hard at Darlene. Darlene nodded just barely. I knew something was going to happen but didn't know what. They trotted up on the stage, smiling like always, and started the record player. It was a great routine. At some points, their feet were flying so close together it was like watching gears on a clock fitting in and out. They got through most of it. Then Marlene stuck her umbrella out in an odd way, and Darlene tripped over it. That was the only time before or since that I saw them make a mistake like that. Darlene tumbled down to the floor. Blood was everywhere. Both her knees and her palms were a mass of red, and her nose looked like a fountain spurting blood.

Marlene yelled, "No!" and threw her arms around Darlene. Mr. Herring ran out from the wings, and a couple of parents ran down from the back of the theater. Mrs. Dunbarton wasn't there that day. The adults tried to lift Darlene, but she threw her arm over Marlene's shoulder and let her sister lead her off the stage. The audience clapped and yelled louder than I had ever heard.

You know the twins won. The Willises didn't even get second or third.

"Do you think Marlene did that on purpose?" I asked Carol while we were walking home.

"No," she said. Then she said, "Maybe. I don't think so. Do you?"

"No," I said, but I wasn't sure. We didn't talk about it again.

The next Saturday, Bobby Erwin came in with his right arm in a sling because he hurt his wrist, he said, and juggled one-handed. He had juggled with both hands many times but not won anything. He won first prize that week. Then, after that, Jolie Johnson brought in her three-legged trick dog and won. The third week after the twins won, it looked like every kid onstage had some kind of hurt. That was when Mr. Herring stopped the talent shows. We didn't see the Willises again.

It was some months later, in the spring, that "the girl in the iron lung" came through town. The school thought it would be an educational experience to teach us about polio. We were told to bring a dime to school to drop in the donation box for polio research, so we could see the girl, and since the bus that carried her was parked only a few blocks away from the school, we were all marched down there. We walked in the front end of the bus and filed past her whooshing metal tube, which had a couple of little windows in it you could look through and see her body. A mirror hung over her face so we could see her, and she could see us. She looked bored. After we saw her, we walked out the rear door, filled with awe at the horror of it, and thinking how it could have been little Joey in the iron lung.

***

Marlene and Darlene hung up their dancing shoes after high school. They both married local boys. Marlene and her husband stayed in Tifton, and Darlene and hers moved to Texas. Sadly, they'd inherited a genetic predisposition for cancer, and both of them died in their fifties, around the same time some of the rest of us, who had just sat back and watched and clapped for them, were coming into our own. It was like they'd worn themselves out with all that dancing and needed an early break.

Max

SUMMER 1953

The Fredericks were the fat family. Of course, we never came right out and said that, in spite of the fact that it would have cost us less breath. Instead, we danced all around it. If we were talking with someone and wanted to refer to the Fredericks, and they were having trouble knowing who we were talking about, we'd say, "You know, she's the history teacher for the eighth grade, and he has the State Farm insurance office down on Main Street." If they still didn't register who we meant, we'd say, "They only have the one boy, Max, in junior high school, who's in Scouts." About that time, most people would say, "Oh, yes. Are they all, um, rather large?" And you'd say yes and both of you would nod in a knowing way and pat yourselves on the back for being nice and not calling them the fat family.

In fact, they were more than "rather large." If the three of them sat, as they often did, in one of the side pews of the Methodist church that were made to accommodate five normal-sized people, or maybe six skinny ones, they took up every inch of space in the seat so that not one hymnal could be wedged between them.

Max was Lowell's age, which was thirteen. Whenever you'd see Max, except at school, he was with his parents, instead of with friends of his own. Mrs. Frederick was always calling our house on the phone and asking if Lowell could come over to work on a Scout project with Max, like she was trying to get Lowell to be Max's buddy, but Lowell wasn't all that interested.

My mother felt sorry for Max. "He can't help it if he's fat," she'd say. "Lowell, it's not going to hurt you to spend an afternoon with the boy. They're real nice people." Sometimes he'd go.

At the beginning of the summer after fifth grade, my mother and I attended the ceremony at the American Legion Hall where the Boy Scouts got awarded badges they'd earned during the year, so we could clap for Lowell. Mr. and Mrs. Frederick went too. They sat in front, grinning and looking about to pop from being so proud of Max. The Scouts who arranged the folding chairs in the hall for the events always set up a couple of special chairs in the front row for the Fredericks. They were sturdier than the regular folding chairs, and everybody else knew who they were for and not to sit in them. The boys wore their khaki uniforms, with broad green sashes where their badges were sewn on in neat rows. Max must have had thirty badges, way more than anybody else. Unfortunately, the sash, running tight across his stomach, made him look even fatter. Lowell only had about six badges on his sash, but it hung loose and graceful over his chest.

After the program, while we were standing around the refreshment table, Mrs. Frederick and my mother chatted while I kept myself busy rearranging the cookies on the trays into fancy patterns. Mrs. Frederick said, "Max's going for his Junior Lifesaving badge next. He's signed up for the class at the swimming pool this summer. Is Lowell going to take the class?"

My mother said, "No, but I think Judy is going to. She finished all the swim classes last summer, and Coach Turner said he'd let her in the lifesaving class, even though she's not really old enough. At least it'll keep her busy, and she's always at the pool anyway." She turned around and saw me playing with the cookies and pulled me away from the table.

Mrs. Frederick bent over to me and said, "We'll look for you there! It's going to be a lot of fun, don't you think?" She talked to me like I was a baby, but I liked her. She was always kind of laughing under her breath, like everything was funny and exciting.

The first day in Junior Lifesaving, Coach Fred Turner, the instructor, who was also the football coach at the high school and had been one of my uncle's college roommates, lined us up on the pool deck, and told us what a motley lot we were, and that he hoped against hope that he could whip us into shape to earn our Junior Lifesaving certificates, but he had doubts. There were four other girls besides me, all of them twelve years old. Max and another boy were thirteen, a third boy was eleven, and I was still ten. My birthday wasn't until September. Size-wise, Max was the biggest by far, and I was the smallest. I don't know how to guess about weights, but Max made more than two of me.

Max's belly stuck out over the waistband of his trunks and bobbled up and down when he walked. That first day, one of the girls looked at his belly and started to giggle. She slapped her hand over her mouth but couldn't keep from snorting through her fingers. Coach Turner came up about an inch from her face and glared like his eyes would burn a hole right into her. The muscles in his jaw drew up tight, he clinched his teeth, and said, one slow word at a time, "We will have none of that behavior in this class. The next outburst from any of you will get your butt tossed out of the pool and out of my class forever!" That ended that.

Mrs. Frederick was the only parent there. She sat outside the chain-link fence as close as she could get to where the class was going on but not close enough to really hear, with all the noise from other kids who weren't in the class splashing around and yelling. She kept smiling and fluttered her fingers in little waves at Max whenever he looked in her direction. You could tell it embarrassed Max, the way he turned his head away from her.

In the first class, we learned how to jump in the pool without going underwater when we saw someone drowning, so we could keep our eyes on him. You stretch out your arms and legs and jump in, and your head stays up. We all got it, but Max had a harder time. When he hit the water, it splashed like he was doing a cannonball, but nobody laughed.

The Fredericks drove past me walking home after the class, and Mrs. Frederick slowed down and called out, "See you tomorrow!"

The class met for an hour every day during the week for several weeks, I don't know how many. But the second day, walking home, Mrs. Frederick stopped and asked me if I wanted a ride as far as their house. They lived about halfway to our house. When I opened the car door, I saw that she had already spread out a towel in the back seat for me to sit on in my wet bathing suit. On the third day, she called me over to get in their car before they left the pool. Mrs. Frederick had a lot of cheery things to say and tried to get Max to talk, but he only mumbled and stared out the window. As soon as we got to their house, Max jumped out of the car as fast as he could, which wasn't all that fast, and ran into the front door, and Mrs. Frederick brought me a glass of ice water before I walked on home. I rode with them every day after that.

One time, after a couple of weeks, Mrs. Frederick asked me if I would come in and wait for her to get some papers she needed to give to my mother, something about Boy Scouts. I was glad to carry the papers to my mother, and I was also curious about the inside of their house. I had wondered if all the furniture was big like they were. It was, but the main thing that smacked me in the face as soon as I stepped into the living room was that pictures of Max were all over the place, dozens of them, from when he was a tiny baby until now. They hung on the walls, they were propped on the mantel, and they covered all the tables. It made me feel a little sorry for Max having that much attention pointed at him and making it hard to hide.

In the living room at my house, we had one big baby picture of Lowell that hung over the sofa. He had won it from the photography studio in town for being judged the "Most Beautiful Baby in Tifton" when he was a little thing. He was a cute-looking baby. We didn't have any pictures of me in the living room, not that I cared. Lowell got tired of my mother telling people about him winning the baby contest, now that he was thirteen, and I was glad I didn't have to deal with that problem.

Mrs. Frederick came back into the living room with the papers for my mother and saw me leaning down to look at the pictures of Max on the coffee table. "Oh, you're looking at Max's pictures," she said.

"You sure have a lot of them," I said.

She chuckled and put her soft fingertips so gently on my cheek it felt like a kiss. "He's the only one we've got, you know? We used to hope maybe we'd have another one, a little girl, but God only gave us Max, and that's blessing enough."

For a moment, I thought about what it would be like to be the Frederick's little girl. I'd be fat like them. We'd have to move to the middle row of pews at the Methodist church because we wouldn't fit on the side row any more, and with all the pictures of me added to the ones of Max, you wouldn't be able to find a place to set down a magazine or a coffee cup in the living room.

Mrs. Frederick asked me to come in a few more times. She gave me some cookies once and showed me a poster map she was drawing of the battlefields of the War Between the States. History of the war was her thing. She said she was working on organizing a club for the United Children of the Confederacy, and would I be interested? I said I'd talk to my mother about it. Another time, she took me in their backyard to show me her roses and insisted that I smell each different type and notice how they were all different. She was always kind to me, and I wished that Lowell would be nicer to Max because I knew that would make her happy.

The class progressed. We had to drag a bag of rocks up from the deep end of the pool and get it over the side onto the deck, and jump in the pool with all our clothes on (with our swimsuits on underneath), and take them off in the water. We mastered the chin carry and the overarm carry and hauled each other around the pool from one end to the other. We learned artificial respiration. I loved it. Coach told us funny stories, and chastised us, and marched around the pool with a whistle that he blew to get us to look at him. He was great. It was a special compliment if he called you a "lazy bum" and said you could do better. He only called you that if you were doing OK. He never called Max a lazy bum but seemed especially careful with him.

Max learned. It just took him a longer time. It got to where the rest of us didn't even think about Max being fat. The worst of it for him was when we had to do things together, like the carry holds. Nobody laughed, or groaned, but you could tell no one wanted to have to try to wrap their arm around his huge belly, or to grab hold of his chin with all that extra fat padding that made it hard to find his chin bones to latch on to.

Coach blew his whistle and yelled, "You don't have any say in who you rescue! People don't come in convenient sizes or shapes. Sometimes you get a scrawny little rat to pull in and you wonder if you're going to break her bones by hanging onto her!" Of course, we all knew he was saying that so he wouldn't have to say Max was fat and we had to learn to save him too.

After that first day when the girl snickered, nobody said a word about Max being fat. But, back in the locker room, I heard the girls whisper about how they worried that they'd be paired up with Max in the final test. I didn't say anything because they were twelve and I was ten, and they didn't talk much to me anyway, but I was worried too. Coach told us a few days before the test that we better be prepared to save *anybody* in the test, that we would not have any more choice about who we saved in the test than we would if we were actual lifeguards at the beach. He said he was going to match us up by pulling names out of a bowl.

The final test for all the swim classes was done in the evening, with the pool lit up. That was so that the parents who worked could come see what we'd learned. They sat or stood around the outside of the chain-link fence. Coach dressed up for the tests in white shorts, a nice yellow shirt, and his dirty buckskin loafers without socks, his whistle hanging around his neck. He carried a clipboard to make notes. The swim classes were first: beginner, intermediate, and advanced. Coach had assistants for the swim classes, and they stayed in the water while the kids went through their paces. There were a lot of them. Then they had some races for the advanced swimmers.

Finally, the Junior Lifesaving group came up. I was nervous, waiting all that time sitting cross-legged against the fence watching the other classes and running through my head what I needed to do. It was a relief to get started. One by one, Coach yelled out instructions to us. "Get that bag of rocks out of the pool! Jump in and keep your head up!" And we'd do what he said. When it came to the exercises we had to do with each other, he made a big show of drawing names out of a paper cup. The first name would be paired with the second, the third with the fourth, and so on. He drew Max's name fifth, and the three of us remaining looked at one another, hoping our name would not be next. Coach pulled the next name and glared at us. "Judy," he called out, and, even though I didn't think he meant to, he sent me a pitying look.

I told myself I could do it. I had hauled him around before with the chin carry and the overarm carry, so I knew I could do that part. It was actually fun, once I got my fingers dug into his chin, to lead him around the pool, pushing up on his butt with my feet if he started to sink. He floated pretty good, so that part was OK.

The problem came when I had to get him out of the pool. I stood on the deck and bobbed him up and down like we were taught before I tried to yank him over the edge, but his belly got hung up on the ledge, and he slipped back in the water. Only the other thirteen-year-old boy had managed, while we were practicing, to get him out of the pool alone. I don't know why I thought I could do it now, but I did think I could if I tried hard enough. I bobbed him up and down again. The whole pool was quiet except for the sound of the water lapping against his big body. That time, when I tried to pull him up and over the edge, he came a little farther, and I think he tried to help me by pushing his knee into the gulley under the edge, but it didn't work. He slipped in again. By the third try, I heard a few people around the pool making some noise, and somebody laughed. I heard someone say, "Like a whale." Coach yelled, "Quiet!," and it stopped.

Somewhere out of the corner of my eye, I saw Mrs. Frederick clinging to the chain-link fence with her fat fingers threaded through the wire, looking worried. I wanted to get Max out of that pool as much as I had ever wanted to do anything—for her and for me, and maybe a little for Max, but I couldn't do it. Coach came over to me and, like he'd done in the lessons when people were trying to get Max out, took hold of Max's arms below where my hands were holding him and helped me pull. Everybody clapped and hooted when he flopped onto the deck.

Max was supposed to keep lying there so I could turn him over and do artificial respiration with him, but he didn't. He got onto his knees for a couple of minutes, puffing like he was worn out. Then he stood up and walked over to the fence where he had left his towel and wrapped it around his waist and kept on walking right out of the gate. He didn't look back. Coach called out, loud enough for Max to hear, but not loud enough for all the watchers to hear, "Max, we're not done yet. Max, you need to stay until we're finished." But Max kept on going. I saw Mr. and Mrs. Frederick leave their place at the fence. Then we saw Max come around from the back of the pool, and they all headed for their car.

Coach coughed and said, like nothing had happened, "OK. Well, let's continue. We've got two more of you bums to show us what you've learned! Get in the water!" But it was different after Max left. I felt really sad for all of us, like we'd all failed in a way, since we didn't all make it through the end to get our certificates. And I felt sad for Mrs. Frederick, and for Max. Since I knew nobody else could get Max out of the pool either, I didn't worry so much that I had failed to do it. I just felt sad.

The next year at school, Mrs. Frederick put out a notice about the United Children of the Confederacy starting up. It was going to be open to any student in junior high who could show they had ancestors who had fought in the war. We all did, of course. I picked up the form from Mr. Jackson's office and brought it home. My mother filled it out, writing in how many of my dead relatives had served in the Confederacy and which divisions they were in and brought it back to Mrs. Frederick in her eighth-grade classroom after school. She acted like she was glad to see me and gave me a quick little hug. That was what I wanted—to know she still liked me. She told me Max was doing OK and that he'd want her to say hello for him. I didn't believe it, but I was glad she said it anyway.

The one UCC meeting I went to, Mrs. Frederick and one of the mothers drove us to a place where there had been a battle in 1863, and walked around telling us which generals had been sitting where on their horses. It wasn't all that interesting to me, and as much as I liked Mrs. Frederick, I didn't go back.

***

Since Max was three years older than me, I didn't have much contact with him after the lifesaving class and only know through my brother what happened with him. He and his parents all died young, or what we'd call "young" now. Mr. Frederick had a heart attack while he was sitting in his insurance office, signing papers with some clients. The ambulance driver who came to get him said he still had a firm grip on his fountain pen when they lifted him onto the stretcher. That was the same year Max went away to college at the University of Alabama. Mrs. Frederick lived to see Max graduate college and complete a PhD in history at Duke University, her alma mater, before she also had a heart attack and died. Max himself had just started teaching at the University of Georgia when he died. He had never married and wasn't yet thirty years old. I don't know the details of his passing.

I do know that the United Children of the Confederacy chapter that Mrs. Frederick started was discontinued after two years due to lack of interest. Apparently, she'd had trouble drumming up much passion for carrying on the war, even though it was less than one hundred years after it had ended.

Lucy
FALL 1953

Lucy's family moved to Tifton in the summer between fifth and sixth grades, when her father got the job to be Tifton's school superintendent. When school started in September, she and I found ourselves in the same classroom. Initially, we connected on our height. We were both tall, so on any occasion of group photography, we were told to go to the back of the pack while the other kids lined up in rows in front of us. We chatted while we waited for the rest to get in place. It was a thin connection, but enough for her to invite me over to her house after school one day.

The Bentleys were from the mountains of North Carolina. They were southerners, but different in some ways from us South Georgia natives. Her parents were tall, slender, and elegant. They carried themselves in a more upright way than my parents or my friends' parents, who seemed to lean in toward the ground. Lawrence, Lucy's father, and Mary Katherine, her mother, nearly always appeared happy. Our parents, even when they were cheerful, bore scars from the Great Depression and the war and had a worried look lurking right behind any happy presentation. The Bentleys were like movie stars while our parents were everyday people, and the Bentleys seemed younger. Lucy had a baby sister which seemed to be evidence of youthfulness and sexuality. It was not that we had any knowledge of sex, but we knew that to have a baby, sex was involved, and we were also sure that our own parents had no familiarity with that subject.

For all of his elegance of bearing, you'd know that Lawrence Bentley was in fact a homely man, if you took the time to study about it. He had a craggy face like Abraham Lincoln's. I recognized the similarity myself before Lucy casually mentioned it, and hinted that her father and Abe Lincoln shared a nobility of character and that it came out in their faces. And they were both in government, as she pointed out. I didn't say it, of course, but I noted that Lucy didn't say anything about the fact that while Abe was president of the whole USA at the time of the country's greatest trial, Lawrence was the school superintendent of a tiny Georgia town in 1953, when the most difficult issue was funding a new football field.

Mary Katherine had mounds of long, curly, auburn hair which she wore pulled back in an unkempt ponytail, a far cry from the "every hair in its place" do that other mothers wore. I thought she was beautiful. And the baby, Brenda, was the cutest thing I had ever seen. She was two years old with a head full of blonde curls and a smile that could break your heart. I loved babies.

I adored the Bentleys, and I must admit to being impressed with Lucy's father's position. Given the insecurity in my own family, having a friend whose father was the school superintendent lent me some badly-needed status. The main thing that Lucy offered in her own right was that she wanted adventure in her life, and said so. I had never thought about naming what I wanted as "adventure," but I was intrigued. At least, Lucy wasn't satisfied with the lives laid upon us by what I was coming to see as a narrow little world. I liked that. We began to spend time together.

"We could be girl detectives," Lucy said, "like Nancy Drew." It was a hot September Saturday. We were walking down 12th Street and going nowhere, just walking.

"Yeah," I agreed in principle. "But we don't have a mystery to solve. Where can we find a mystery? Nothing ever happens here."

She frowned, annoyed, I thought, with my practical observation. "We have to look for the mystery," she said, like it was simple as pie to just glance around and see a mystery bubbling up in this town where everything was known, everything was predictable, where a five-year-old child could tell you who was who and what was what, and how tomorrow was going to play out.

We had come to the A&P grocery store, and both of us had a few coins. We went into the store and spent some time choosing all-day suckers, five cents each. I liked the grape-swirled ones, and Lucy was partial to cherry. Before putting them in our mouths, we carefully folded the paper wrappers and put them in our pockets to wrap up the suckers at the point where our tongues got sore from working on them.

Back on the sidewalk, Lucy stopped in her tracks. "I know!" she said. "We can spy on Mrs. Penny!"

Mrs. Penny was our civics teacher. She was young. Most of the teachers were old and had been in their positions since they were born, as far as we knew, and Mrs. Penny had just this year started teaching. And she was expecting a baby. Most women who were pregnant (or "p.g.," as my mother said to be modest) kept themselves close to home. I had not seen a p.g. teacher before and had overheard hints that it was unseemly for a lady in her condition to be out in the public teaching children.

I removed the blob of sugar from my mouth. "Why would we spy on Mrs. Penny?" I wanted to know.

"Because I know where she lives," Lucy said. "I saw her going into that apartment building on 16th Street last week. Then I saw the light go on in the downstairs right-hand side. It had to be her going in and turning it on!"

I didn't stop to address the fact that Lucy knowing where Mrs. Penny lived was not a justification for spying on her. Lucy was so pleased with her powers of deduction that I didn't want to spoil it for her.

Later that night, when we were supposed to be playing gin rummy in Lucy's bedroom, we snuck out the back door and walked the two blocks to Mrs. Penny's apartment building, a redbrick fourplex. The whole top floor was dark, but the bottom floor had lights blazing on both sides. From her recent reconnaissance, Lucy knew which side was Mrs. Penny's.

We slunk along the walkway from the sidewalk toward the front door and then squatted down under a camellia bush by the stoop. The windows were open, and we could hear muffled sounds of Mrs. Penny and a man we guessed to be her husband, talking. It was weirdly thrilling to be listening to them even though we couldn't tell what they were saying. It was also terrifying. I kept expecting Sheriff Tom Anderson to drive up in his government car and point his gun at us and take us to jail, where we'd spend the night, and Sally Ann would bring us our breakfast on a tray in the morning.

Lucy had a small notebook and a stub of pencil. She scribbled in the book.

"What are you writing?" I whispered.

"Notes."

After she stuck the notebook in the pocket of her jeans, Lucy said, "Let's go!" We got onto our knees and crawled under azalea bushes along the side of the building. Lucy stepped on a twig and broke it, making a loud crack. The man said, "What's that?" and looked out the window.

I quit breathing for a long time while I imagined trying to explain to my and Lucy's parents about playing Nancy Drew. I figured my parents would have to forgive me eventually, but Lucy's parents were not bound to. I'd miss them and little Brenda.

When it got quiet in the Pennys' apartment, Lucy and I slithered back out to the street and stood up, acting like we were out for an evening stroll.

"I'm not doing that again," I said. "That was stupid." I was still not sure that Sheriff Anderson would not drive up alongside us with his sirens blaring.

"Why not?" Lucy said. "It was fun. We didn't hurt anybody." She seemed excited about the whole thing. "Look at my notes."

The scribbles in the little notebook outlined what we had done: "Got to Penny's house at 8:15 p.m., Sept. 27. Lights were on downstairs. Overheard conversation."

"So what if they were talking?" I said. "What if we got caught?"

"It's all right," she said. "My daddy is the school superintendent."

I couldn't argue with that. I didn't know how it worked, but if she was so sure she was protected from the consequences of her behavior, maybe she was. I wasn't.

For a while after spying on Mrs. Penny, I stayed away from Lucy. When she asked me to come over, I'd make up some excuse not to do it. It was probably a month later, close to Halloween, when I saw Mrs. Bentley and the baby in their car when she came to pick up Lucy from school. Mrs. Bentley smiled her big smile and called me over. Brenda was in her lap, waving her hands and bouncing like a frog. I was playing with her when Lucy came out, and before they left, I agreed to come to her house the next day after school.

"I've got an idea," Lucy whispered, almost as soon as I came into her house. Her parents were not there. "We can crawl out the window of the cloakroom! Here's my plan. I will say I don't feel well and that I need to lie down. Mrs. Bowen will tell me to go to the cot in the cloakroom. I'll say I need you to come with me in case I need anything, and she'll say OK. Then we'll go in there and shut the doors and crawl out the window. We can go down to the A&P and get a sucker or something and come back!"

"Why are you whispering?" I asked.

"I don't know," she said.

The plan appealed to me more than spying on Mrs. Penny. It had a goal, it made sense in a way, and it didn't hurt anybody. I thought we could pull it off, and Lucy would be satisfied that we were having an adventure. Tomorrow was the day.

We got permission to go to the cloakroom as planned. Lucy climbed out the window first. The window was so high that for a moment, she hung by her fingertips before dropping about a foot onto the ground. "It's not far," she whispered up to me. "I'll hold around your waist until you land."

So I was hanging there by my fingers when I heard Corky Jackson, the principal, chuckling softly. I dropped to the ground and looked up to see him standing a few feet away from us.

"Do you girls want to climb back in through the window, or do you want to come around and go in the door?" he asked. You could tell he was working hard to keep from busting full-out laughing.

I wondered what was coming next, if he was going to be calling our parents, or to tell Mrs. Bowen, and if I'd get spanked when I got home or suspended from school. I didn't know why he was laughing, but I tried to act like it was a normal thing to ask, like if he wanted to know if we were eating lunch in the lunchroom or had brought our lunch that day. "I guess I will climb in the window," I said. "I'm a good climber."

Lucy pulled at her skirt to smooth it back down. "I will also climb in the window," she said, sounding huffy. Then she added, "Mr. Jackson, do you know my daddy is the school superintendent?"

Mr. Jackson quit laughing. "I do know that, Lucy. Do you want me to call him for you? You can tell him about this yourself if you want to."

Lucy stepped back. Her chin started to quiver and tears seeped out of the corners of her eyes. "No," she said. "You don't have to call him." After a moment, she added, "I'm sorry," in a soft voice.

"Do you need a boost to get back up there?" Mr. Jackson asked. He didn't wait for us to answer but came over and made a stirrup with his hands for us to step into to reach the window ledge.

We didn't hear another word about the escape attempt. Mrs. Bowen acted like nothing had happened when Lucy and I went back into the classroom, and Lucy said she was feeling better. Lucy sat at her desk and made some notes in her book, but I didn't ask to see them. I waited anxious days for my mother to tell me that Corky Jackson had called her and for her to lay down some serious punishment, but it never happened. It was weeks later before I understood that Corky had never told anyone. I was probably more chastened by the suspense than I would have been if Corky had told but not Lucy.

She did not stop her sleuthing and eventually hit upon the one real mystery in Tifton. We were at recess about a month after our escape attempt, and Lucy made a big production about pulling me over to the edge of the playground away from the other kids.

"I found this vacant house!" she whispered. She was really excited. "It's just a couple of blocks from your grandparents' house."

"I know which one," I told her. I did know. Everybody in town knew. "It's Brother Norris' house, and he's in the mental hospital."

"Oh," she said, like that didn't matter to her. "Well, one of the windows in the back is unlocked! We could get in and just kind of look around. We wouldn't bother anything."

The bell rang for recess to be over and we had to go back inside, so I told her I'd meet her after school.

It was on a Friday afternoon in early November, just beginning to get chilly, which felt good after the long, sweaty summer. School was out for the weekend, and we decided to walk over to the A&P to get all-day suckers, which were becoming so much a habit that my tongue stayed blue most of the time, and also tender, from the constant licking on them.

While we were walking, I explained to Lucy as well as I could about Brother, but since she hadn't been born here, she didn't really understand. Understanding required more than just the simple facts, which in this case were (1) that Brother Norris had been in the army in the war, (2) that a German hand grenade had blown off the top of his skull, (3) that the doctors at the VA hospital in Albany had installed a steel plate in his head where the missing bone had been.

After his return to Tifton following the war, Brother had lived in his parents' house. From that time on, he did nothing but sit in the afternoons on the porch in a rocker beside his mother.

His father was already dead before Brother stepped one foot on foreign soil, so it was just him and his mother living there. Because of the steel plate, Brother could never get excited, or jump around, or run, or laugh more than a little chuckle, or his brain might push up against the steel plate, and he would be a goner. So people were quiet and moved slow around him, and I always wondered what was the point of him even being alive if that was all he had to look forward to.

Then, two years ago, Mrs. Norris died.

After that, Brother got put in the mental hospital in Milledgeville because there wasn't anybody to look after him, even if he was a war hero. The house still belonged to Brother. There weren't any relatives, and no one wanted to say he'd never come home, him being a war hero and all, so the house just stood there.

"They just left the house like it was the day he left it," I said. "On account of him being a war hero. Then, about a year ago, people started saying it was haunted. Lovey and Pet Davis said maybe Mr. and Mrs. Norris were roaming around the house looking for Brother. Mr. Rigley, Anna's daddy, who had also seen combat in the war, said it might be shades of German soldiers that Brother shot and killed before the top of his head got blown off, looking for Brother, to get him back for killing them." A lot of the fathers who had been in combat came home odd.

"Have you seen inside it?" Lucy took the little notebook out of her pocket and started scribbling.

"I used to go over there with my grandmother to visit Mrs. Norris and Brother. You had to be very still and not laugh or talk loud. Brother seemed nice. He liked to play checkers, but if you won, you didn't make a fuss about it. You'd just whisper, 'I think I won.' Then, when he won, he'd do the same thing."

"Why do people say there are ghosts in the house?" Lucy scratched away at her notes.

"Mrs. Frederick saw a light in the window one time," I said. "And, another time, the door was open. When Sheriff Tom Anderson went to check, nobody was there."

The more I told Lucy about Brother and his house, the more I wanted to see inside it again for myself, even though to think about it made goose bumps jump up all over my arms and reminded me that I'd followed Lucy into places I shouldn't have been before. I ignored the reminder.

We decided to walk by the house right after we bought our candy and check out the window that Lucy said was unlocked.

"You really like to crawl in and out of windows," I observed.

"I've been reading the Hardy Boys," she answered. "They are for boys, but Mrs. Mitchell at the library said I could read them too. They're all the time getting in and out of places through windows."

From the outside, the house looked pretty much like it did when I went over there with Mama, except that the yard was overgrown. The grass needed to be cut bad, and a confederate jasmine vine that used to twist in and out through a lattice at the side of the porch had long since leapt off that lattice and wound its way along the porch railings like a wild thing. Some camellias at the corners of the house had grown twice as big as they used to be. Unkempt as they were, they were covered with buds this time of year. Tall grass poked up between the bricks on the walkway from the sidewalk to the house. It was easy to tell nobody lived there, or if they did, it was a person who didn't care much about keeping a civilized yard.

Lucy and I checked around to make sure we were not being looked at before we trooped through the tall grass to the back of the house. Lucy pointed out the unlocked window. A concrete block stood on end right underneath the window where she had left it. I climbed up on the block and tested the window, which slid right up.

"See!" she said. "It'll be so easy!"

"What are we waiting for?" I asked. "Let's just do it now!"

Lucy didn't need to be persuaded. "Now is as good a time as any," she said.

The overgrown bushes made a cover for us. The neighbors couldn't see into the backyard. I guessed Mrs. Frederick had seen a light in the front of the house because the back was like a jungle in a *Tarzan* movie. I didn't even try to be quiet or to hide what I was doing.

There was a screen on the window, but it was not latched and was hanging at an angle. As soon as I shoved at it, it came crashing down on the floor inside. The window was so low that I just threw my leg up and got my foot inside. I ducked my head to get under the window and then pulled myself up and inside the house. Then I was standing in the kitchen. A whole flood of memories came over me about the last day I had been there, the day of Mrs. Norris's funeral. After we watched her get lowered into the grave at Oak Ridge Cemetery, I had come back to the house with Mama and Papa and a bunch of other people to drink punch and eat little sandwiches. Mama loved funerals. I remembered how lost Brother looked that day and how his suit didn't fit him and how he didn't say a word, which everyone thought was strange. They were whispering about how he had not been right since the war.

"Get me in!" Lucy called. I had about forgotten her. I got hold of her hands and pulled her through the window. The first thing she did was to sit down on a chair and start writing in her notebook. I kept looking around trying to remember more about how the kitchen used to be.

In most ways, it didn't look like anything was different, except that there was a lot of dust that wasn't there before. The white metal kitchen table with the red rim around the sides and the red plastic-covered chairs were just like the ones we had at my house. Little ceramic chickens were everywhere. Chickens decorated the canister set and the paper-napkin holder. The refrigerator door was open, with nothing inside. I opened a couple of cabinets and saw dishes but no food.

"What are you looking for?" Lucy asked. I told her I didn't know, but I kept opening doors and drawers. Lucy followed along behind me, and for once, she seemed more timid than me.

Then something seemed odd, like it didn't belong. A jar of Jif peanut butter and a wrapper of Sunshine saltine crackers appeared right behind a stack of mixing bowls in a cabinet at the side of the stove. Mrs. Norris wouldn't have kept her peanut butter down there. I pointed this out to Lucy, who just said, "I see." She made some notes in her notebook. Then she said we should leave. We could come back another time like we had planned.

The second time we went in the house, we wandered through the other rooms. Like the kitchen, all the furniture was in place and covered with dust, but it was still neat underneath the dust. In the room we guessed was Brother's, on account of a picture of him in his army uniform and another one of him with a group of other army men hanging on the wall, the bed was not made. "He must have left in a hurry," Lucy said. I couldn't remember anything about the day Brother got taken away except that Mama said it was sad.

By our third visit, we had our breaking-and-entering procedure down pat. By then, it seemed so routine that it didn't even feel like we were doing anything wrong, like the house belonged to us in a way. It was the Saturday after Thanksgiving and already cold enough for us to be wearing our jackets, which made us a little bulky to pull through the window, but we made it. Inside the house was even colder. We sat down at the kitchen table so Lucy could jot down her notes. She was hunched over the notebook, and I was slapping my hands together to get them warm, just waiting for her to finish when I looked up and there, standing in the doorway, was Brother.

"Don't yell." I said to Lucy. "Don't jump. You can't make a lot of noise."

Lucy looked at me like I was crazy, which was what I probably sounded like. "What?" she said.

"Brother is here," I said.

Then she realized I was staring behind her and turned around and looked. It didn't matter what I had told her. She shrieked, "Oh, no!" and jumped up.

I grabbed her, shushing her and holding onto her. "It's OK," I said. I didn't really know if it was OK, but I didn't want anything to do with Brother's brain beating up against that steel plate and him falling over dead.

Brother just stood there grinning. "I thought somebody'd been rummaging around in my house," he said. "I didn't know if it was somebody dangerous, or what, but I don't think y'all are that dangerous, are you?" Then he leaned over and studied us up close. I had my arms wrapped around Lucy. She was trembling and had wet her pants. "Why, you're a little Ireland, aren't you?" he asked me.

"I'm Mrs. Tennie Ireland's granddaughter," I said. "I used to come with her to visit your mother, and you and I would play checkers, remember?" I said.

"Yes," Brother said. "I do." He sat down. He was wearing blue jeans and a pajama top. "You promise me you won't tell anybody I'm here. OK?"

"Yes," Lucy said. "We promise. We won't tell a fly. We need to leave now." She looked like she was going to cry.

But Brother wasn't ready for us to leave. "Don't be afraid. I'm not going to hurt you," he said. "Please don't leave. I need some help."

I didn't know what we could do to help him. We were just eleven-year-old girls, but it was like he thought we could, like we were grown up. Then Lucy, wet pants and all, pulled herself up and away from my arms, and said, "How can we help?" like this was what she had been waiting for all along.

"I need a lawyer," he said. "They got me in a place for crazy people, and I ain't crazy."

"How did you get out to come here?" Lucy asked him.

"Oh, I sneak out from time to time, hitchhike home and stay a few days, then I sneak back. They don't ever know. Or if they do, they don't want to admit I outsmarted them, so they don't tell anybody."

Brother didn't look crazy. He didn't act crazy. He just looked tired and sad. His hair was cut too short, and his skin looked too white, like he didn't get in the sun enough.

"My daddy's second cousin is a lawyer," I said. "He's got an office on Main Street next to the Myron Hotel. You can go see him."

"Well," Lucy said, "my daddy is the school superintendent. He can help you!"

Lucy and I told our parents that same day that we had met Brother near the A&P and that he needed a lawyer, and why. We asked them not to make him go back to the mental hospital but just to talk with him, and they did.

Between D. C. Ireland, Esq., and Mr. Lawrence Bentley, Tifton school superintendent, and the combined efforts of the members of the American Legion, Brother Norris got released from the state mental hospital in Milledgeville and moved back into his parents' house before Christmas. He mowed the grass and pruned the jasmine and the camellias, and he repaired the window screens so no more kids could invade. Sometimes, when Lucy and I walked by his house, he called out to us, and we went up and sat a little while with him on his porch. I heard him laugh a few times, right out loud like that steel plate didn't bother him anymore.

Lucy threw away her notebook, and I never heard her mention Nancy Drew or the Hardy Boys again.

***

After high school, Lucy went to college in New York to study education. She married a man she met there and stayed in the city, teaching, for years. I didn't keep up with her, and she didn't come to the reunions until the fortieth. That was the first time I saw her after graduation. She had divorced her New York husband and married another one who moved back to the South with her. She lives in a suburb of Macon, Georgia now and writes opinion pieces with a liberal slant for her local newspaper.

To write such a piece in Macon bears an entirely different weight and requires a lot more courage than it does to do the same thing where I live in Northern California, and it is something to be greatly admired.

So far as I know, Lucy's career in crime ended (as did mine) with the breaking and entering at Brother Norris' house.

When I left Tifton, Brother Norris was living independently in his home. I don't know any further news of him, except that he has surely joined his parents in the Oak Ridge Cemetery by now.

Betty Lou
FALL 1954

Betty Lou was Carol's cousin on the other side of her family. If I am honest, and I try to be, I was always jealous of Betty Lou. I wanted to be sure I was Carol's favorite cousin, and just to know she had another cousin the same age as us was a burr between my toes. I didn't let it show, but it was there. Betty Lou and her brother, Harold, lived on their parents' great big farm out in the county, and we didn't see much of them. So, it wasn't much of a problem until seventh grade when Betty Lou got bused into town to attend school with us.

Carol's family had moved back to Tifton in September of that year, which made me really happy. Then she and I were both assigned to Mrs. Lassiter's homeroom, which made me almost giddy. I figured we'd be able to go back to how we were before she moved away, and we were little kids running around not thinking about much except having a good time. Then Betty Lou showed up in our classroom a week into the school year, and my hopes of turning back the clock disappeared for good.

Betty Lou, for all her family's land and money, was a country girl. All the girls and boys who joined our class in seventh grade after going to the little schools in the county looked and acted "country." Their clothes were different, for one thing. Some of the boys wore overalls. The ones who wore jeans had them pulled up around their waists and fastened with a belt, while the town boys wore Levi's that sat low on their hips without a belt. The country girls wore shirtwaist dresses, with limp skirts, instead of blouses and full skirts with crinolines that made our skirts stand like Scarlett O'Hara's. That's what we town girls wore. A few of the country girls were Nazarenes and had never in their lives cut their hair, which they pinned up in weird styles that screamed *country!* We town girls wore pony tails. The way the country kids talked and acted was different too. You could spot country kids from the far end of the long hallway at school, and if you weren't completely sure, the minute they opened their mouths, you were.

I didn't set out to be mean to Betty Lou. My life was complicated enough right then. My family had had to sell our house to pay off debts from the failure of the hardware store Daddy bought after he quit the post office. We had moved in with Mama and Papa, which was not the same as just visiting with them. I slept in a tiny room, hardly big enough for the twin bed, next to their bedroom with Mama snoring like a freight train every night. My parents said it was temporary until they found another house they could rent until things got better enough to buy one, but it wasn't clear when that would happen. I had started my periods, and I hated the mess and the pain of it, which seemed totally unfair since boys didn't have to go through that. Being twelve years old was not much fun. Most days, I wanted to be a little kid again and to have whatever degree of stability my family had had when I was younger. So, all things considered, I needed every friend I could get and should have bent over backward to be nice to Betty Lou, and I did try.

At first it was OK that it was a little embarrassing to buddy up with her at school. If one of the other girls gave me a funny look when I was standing around with her, I'd say how she was Carol's cousin (which I thought would let them know I didn't have much of a choice about the matter), and if I could think of a way, I'd let them know her family had money. Maybe I'd say how they had a new car, or horses. I thought that she would catch on to how to talk and dress more like us, but she didn't seem to realize she needed to. Then the whole thing about Robert E. Lee came up.

In seventh grade, we studied Georgia history, which involved studying the Civil War. We were taught that while there were some Yankee people, like the ones who had written our textbooks, who made a point that the war was about slavery, the true fact was that the war was about the industrial North versus the agrarian South, and about states that were willing to give over power to the federal government versus states that wanted to make their own decisions. We were taught that the slave owners in the South were kind to their slaves and treated them like their own children, only maybe like children who were not as bright and capable as their white children. We were taught that the South, if it had not been for the war, would have freed the slaves on their own if given a bit more time. We were taught that black people were not ready or able to run their own lives without the help of white people even yet. We were taught that Robert E. Lee was the finest example of manhood who had ever lived, short of Jesus, and that William Tecumseh Sherman was the personification of evil. We were taught that Ulysses S. Grant was a drunk and a coward, the worst president ever to stumble into the office.

If any of us at the time questioned what we were taught, I don't know about it. The teacher had said that's the way it was, so to question her would have been the same as questioning the multiplication tables. I did think about Rosa and Baby, though, and knew for sure they were as bright and capable as any white people in my acquaintance.

At some point, Mrs. Webb, the history teacher, assigned us homework to gather stories about people in our families who had gone through the war and to be able to tell those stories the next day. Betty Lou waved her hand around like she was trying to flag down a bus. "I am related to Robert E. Lee!" she crowed. You'd have thought she was bragging that her family had single-handedly brought about peace on earth. "My daddy is named after him, Robert E. Lee!" She pointed at Carol. "Carol is related to him too! Just like me!" Carol slunk down in her desk and looked out the window.

That night after dinner, I asked my parents about our people in the war. Mama and Papa had already gone to bed. My mother reminded me that her great-grandfather, John B. Mitchell, had been a colonel in the war, and that there was a statue of him in full military dress on his grave in Crisp County. My father said that all the Ireland and Hendrix (Mama's family) men who were neither too old, over sixty-five, or too young, under twelve, had fought in the war.

Then my daddy, I don't know why, moved on to talk about the more recent war. "In World War II, all four of us Ireland boys served on active duty, unlike in some families where the men were draft dodgers." He lowered the newspaper he was reading enough to look over the top of it at my mother. She glared at him.

"What's a draft dodger?" I asked.

My mother said, "Elwyn." She would say your name like that when she was warning you to stop talking about something.

My daddy ignored her and plowed right ahead. "That's men who do anything they can to skip out on their duty to the country, like go to work in the shipyards, or claim to have disabilities, or say their families can't survive if they aren't there."

I could tell there was more going on between them than talking about who was in what war. They were both quiet for a few minutes. Then my mother said, "My brothers worked in the shipyards in the war. It was important work and nothing to be ashamed of." She got up and left the room.

The next day, before I went to school, I asked Mama if she could tell me more about her family and the Civil War. She said she remembered a story from her mother, Bama, who had lived up in the northwest corner of North Georgia, almost Tennessee. When the war came, the men all joined up with J. E. B. Stuart. They didn't have any slaves to speak of, but they felt like they needed to defend their land from the Yankees.

Bama told Mama that her family had a man named Benjamin and his wife (Mama couldn't remember her name), who lived with them in a shed room attached to the back of the house, but that nobody ever thought of them as slaves. She said that people in North Georgia didn't think about black people the way people in South Georgia did. I wondered how Benjamin and his wife thought of themselves. Anyway, when Sherman came down, Bama's mother had only three laying hens and a milk cow. She had been left on the farm with her five-year-old boy, and Benjamin and his wife and she didn't know when or if her husband would come home. So when she got word that Sherman's bandit scum were close at their heels, Benjamin and his wife took the hens and the cow into the woods to hide. After a week, after Sherman had done his damage and left, they came back and stayed on with Bama's mother until her husband returned. I liked Mama's story better but thought my mother's great-grandfather in a statue sounded more important, so that's the story I decided to tell at school.

Mrs. Webb went through the class one by one, having us stand up and say something about our Civil War ancestors. Most of us covered the subject in a matter of minutes, but when Betty Lou's turn came, she opened her notebook and pulled out pages of typed information and pictures. Then she proceeded to read the notes and pass the pictures around the room until the class was over. While she was talking, other people in the class shot looks at one another that said that Betty Lou was a total nut, in addition to being a country girl.

That day at school during recess, I saw Sally Ann sidle up to Betty Lou and felt sick to my stomach because I knew Sally Ann would be up to no good and that I needed to look after Betty Lou, whether I wanted to or not. I went over to them in time to hear Sally Ann say, "You must be so proud of being related to Robert E. Lee!"

Betty Lou said, "Well, yes, I am. In my family, we've studied all about him."

Sally Ann said, "It's too bad they didn't name you Roberta, so everybody who met you would know without you having to tell them."

Betty Lou still didn't get it that Sally Ann was making fun of her. She just said, "Yes, it would have been nice. I imagine they didn't think about it."

"Maybe we should just call you Roberta from now on," Sally Ann added, smiling so sweet you'd think she had just been awarded a halo. There are some twelve-year-old girls who are awful people and should be kept locked up in a pit until they get more caring about other people.

I guess about then Sally Ann felt like she needed to come down even harder, since her insults seemed to bounce off Betty Lou like rubber balls. She said, "That's a nice dress. I like it. Where did you get it?" Betty Lou had on the ugliest dress you could ever think of that day, blue polka dots with a skinny tie around the waist and a little white Peter Pan collar.

She still didn't get it. "I'm glad you like it," Betty Lou said. "My mama bought it from the Sears catalogue. I've got another one, a green one, just like it."

Sally Ann said, "Oh, I think I'll get some like yours!"

I could have given Sally Ann a "stop it" look. I could have taken Betty Lou's arm and pulled her away. There were a dozen things I could have done that I didn't do. Instead, I grinned at Sally Ann and walked away, leaving Betty Lou thinking Sally Ann wanted to be her best friend.

I walked home with Carol that afternoon. "Betty Lou thinks Sally Ann is going to invite her to her party," Carol said.

"I don't think so," I said.

Carol said, "Yeah, I told her not to count on it, but she didn't believe me." Carol and I didn't even know if we were going to be invited.

The most important thing in the world at that time, for the girls and maybe the boys, but I'm not sure about the boys, was getting an invitation to Sally Ann's party. We had known about it for weeks. The party was going to be big, so it seemed like most of us would get invitations, but a few would be left out. The worst thing possible would be to not get an invitation, which would mean you were nobody. We didn't know when the invitations were going to be sent out, but every day after school, we looked through the mail hoping to find one waiting for us.

Carol didn't worry much about the party. She had only been back in Tifton a few months and didn't care what anybody else thought about her. She knew she was somebody anyway, but I didn't know I was.

Well, Betty Lou kept going with the Robert E. Lee thing. It was like any little chance she got, she brought up again how she was related to him and what a great man he was and how proud she was to be a part of his family. She didn't seem to be able to understand that people were tired of it, even when Carol flat-out told her.

Sally Ann called her Roberta every once in a while, which got a snicker from the other kids. A few of the other kids called her Roberta too. I was sitting with Kathy Rigley at lunch when she called across the table, "Hey, Roberta, where's Traveller?" We all knew that Lee's horse was named Traveller.

Betty Lou acted like she didn't hear and just said, "What?" The lunchroom lady came in then and told us to be quiet, but people were giggling. I felt like I had to do something, so I told Kathy to stop teasing Betty Lou, but I wished I didn't have to keep taking care of her. She had brought all this on herself, after all, with the Robert E. Lee business.

So the day Sally Ann called me about the invitations, I was pretty fed up with Betty Lou. Sally Ann said, "I'm mailing my invitations tomorrow, and I need to ask you something."

I said, "OK." I figured that if she was telling me about the invitations, I was going to get one. I hadn't been sure, so it was a big relief.

She said, "I'm inviting you and Carol, but I don't want to invite Betty Lou. Andi said I should invite her because she'll get her feelings hurt if I don't. If I can tell Andi you think it's all right for me not to, then I don't have to."

"I don't know," I said, but I said it real slow and dragged out, so Sally Ann would understand I really didn't want to have to deal with Betty Lou at the party, but I didn't want to say so. Then I added, "I guess it's up to you who you invite."

Sally Ann said, "OK. I won't invite her. I'll tell Andi that you think it's all right."

As soon as I hung up the phone, I felt like I was the worst person in the world. I thought about Betty Lou learning that the rest of us had invitations and she didn't, and how sad she'd be that Robert E. Lee had not gotten her a high place in the seventh-grade social order. I thought about how mad Carol would be at me if she knew what I'd said to Sally Ann and hoped to the Lord that she'd never find out.

It all happened like I thought it would. As soon as she realized that the rest of us had gotten our invitations and she hadn't, Betty Lou was like my mother's angel food cake that was in the oven and folded right up on itself when I slammed the door. She didn't come to school for a couple of days, and when she came back, she hardly spoke to anyone except Carol and me. Then she started saying how she never wanted to go to the party anyway and was glad she hadn't been invited.

The high point of the party was getting the invitation. After that, everything about it was painful. Carol decided not to go when she found out Betty Lou was not invited, so I had to go with Roxanne Cook, who wasn't any fun. My mother thought I should have a new dress, but we couldn't afford one, so she cut down one of my aunt's. It looked OK, but I knew it was a hand-me-down and felt weird wearing it.

The American Legion hall, where the party was, was decorated with pink crepe-paper streamers and balloons. There weren't any games, so the whole bunch of us hung around the refreshment table and drank pink punch and ate cookies until they were all gone. I guess Andi hadn't expected us to have such big appetites.

Andi and Sheriff Anderson played records and tried to get us to dance, but we didn't know how to. Finally, two of the boys asked Sally Ann and Kathy to dance, so they shuffled around in one spot holding hands while the rest of us girls lined up against one wall, and the boys lined up against another one. I felt miserable, like my dress wasn't right, or my hair, or nobody liked me anyway, and wished with all my heart that one of the boys would ask me to dance. Dewayne Ellis did, but he was just my friend and a sissy boy to boot, so it didn't count. Looking around, I could tell most of the others felt as terrible as I did until a streamer fell off the ceiling, and Tommy Waldrop grabbed it. He ran around the room waving it, and the boys chased him, pulling off more streamers as they went until Tommy fell into the punch bowl, and it crashed onto the floor, sending glass shards to every corner of the room. After that, Roxanne said her stomach hurt and she wanted to go home, so we used the phone in the office and called her mother to come get us. I was happy to leave.

Carol didn't know, but I could tell she suspected that I'd had something to do with Betty Lou not getting invited. She got real cool toward me. Then she asked Betty Lou to spend the night with her and didn't ask me. Before, if Betty Lou was at her house, I was there too. Since I was living right next door at Mama and Papa's, I saw Betty Lou come and saw her leave the next day. I was so upset I wrote Carol a note that said, "You are hereby no longer my cousin. Signed, Judy Ireland."

When I gave it to her at school, she read it, and crumpled it up and said, "This is silly and stupid. You can't not be my cousin, no matter what you write." I glared at her, but secretly I was happy to hear her response. It was comforting to know we'd always be cousins, no matter what.

Betty Lou joined the girls' basketball team after the party. A lot of the farm girls were on the basketball team, and she fit right in there. She seemed more relaxed, and I never heard her talk about R. E. Lee anymore.

It took a long time for Carol and me to get back to being best friends again. When we did, in eighth grade, we just eased into it. In the meantime, I got to know the new Yankee girl, and that was a good thing.

***

After high school, Betty Lou went to the community college for a couple of years before she married a young man whose family had a farm out near her parents' place. The marriage was brief but lasted long enough for her to get a son out of the arrangement. I didn't have direct contact with her after high school. She and a lot of the people who stayed in Tifton didn't even attend the reunions to catch up with the rest of us and say hello. Carol told me, though, that Betty Lou continued her interest in R. E. Lee and became heavily immersed in the world of genealogy, to the point where the dead seemed more real to her than the living.

Linda

SPRING 1955

It ran like a red-hot stream through our blood to hate the Yankees. We weren't supposed to say "hate" about anybody, but I guess the preacher, and maybe God himself, made an exception where Yankees were concerned.

We didn't hate any other groups of people. We certainly didn't hate black people. We didn't know enough to see them as our full-fledged brothers and sisters, but we didn't hate them. We didn't hate Jews. There were two Jewish families in Tifton: the Cohens, who owned Belk department store, and the Goldsteins, who owned the Big Store. As far as my mother was concerned, the Jews were just like us, except that they had to drive forty miles to Albany to go to church, and their church was on Saturday instead of Sunday.

We didn't hate Germans. Clarence Norris came back from the war with a German bride. One of my uncles made a comment about her being a Nazi, and my father said in a flash, "War's been over for nine years! She seems like a nice girl, and the cleanest person you could ever hope to meet—scrubs the house night and day." I'm not sure about the Japanese, but I can't remember anybody ever saying a bad word about them except Walt Disney in the cartoons, and he wasn't from Tifton. Of course, there weren't any Japanese or any other Asian people in our town for us to know whether we liked them or not.

All our bad feelings were aimed at the Yankees. It was like there was a school for us when we were babies, before we left the hospitals where we were born, where we were taught how irredeemable these people were. When I was about five or six, just beginning to read on my own, I got a book on Abraham Lincoln from the library and walked the block and a half back to Mama and Papa's to read it. It was a picture book, big pictures with a few lines of writing on the bottom of each page. I didn't know who Lincoln was, but I fell in love with him as I read the book, from the stories about him growing up in a log cabin, reading by candlelight, growing up to be president, and freeing black people, whom I had not known needed freeing.

Papa, my grandfather, who hardly ever opened his mouth except to fork food into it, walked by and saw the book and said, "He was a Yankee."

Already, five years old, I understood that one of the worst things in the world was a Yankee. I offered, "He was the president."

"President of the Union!" Papa snapped.

I was sad about this news. I deeply admired Abraham Lincoln from reading the book and now had to wrestle with my feelings. I had to believe Papa, but I didn't want to.

A few years later, my loving daddy told us about playing harmless jokes on Yankees who stopped at his service stations. He had bought three service stations after the hardware store failed and was trying hard as he could to make a living at running them. A lot of Yankees stopped for gas at the one on Highway 41, driving to Florida for their vacations. We figured anybody from north of the Mason-Dixon Line was a Yankee. Daddy engaged them while he pumped gas or cleaned their windshields. He loved to talk. So the day one of the Yankees asked him about peanut trees and what they looked like, Daddy pointed at a dogwood. "There's one right there! We just finished picking the last of the peanuts last week. If you'd been here then, you could have gotten some for yourself."

Of course, we all knew that peanuts grew underground, so we got a big laugh about how stupid Yankees were. It was surprising because Daddy never made fun of anybody else, but he felt just fine doing it to Yankees.

Mrs. Andrews, Tifton's school music teacher, went to Philadelphia to a Fred Waring class for chorus directors. She was a gifted teacher, funny and demanding, and always brought home first-place ribbons from the district for chorus competitions. When she came back from up North, she told us bits and pieces here and there about her experience, which confirmed our beliefs. Yankees were rude. They'd push you on the sidewalk and never say "excuse me." They had terrible table manners, turned their forks upside down, and kept their elbows on the table while they ate. They were loud and had no sense of humor.

No Yankees lived in Tifton, so when we heard sometime before Easter that a Yankee girl had just moved to Tifton and was going to be in Miss Shepard's seventh-grade class, we were all interested. I had never seen a Yankee. I couldn't imagine a twelve-year-old girl having traits that would live up to the stories I had heard. She'd have to be rude and stupid and have a voice like somebody shaking a can full of rocks.

The night after I first heard that the Yankee girl would be in seventh grade, I mentioned that fact to my daddy. He was sitting in his chair reading the paper but put it down to listen to me. "A little Yankee girl," he said in a sad kind of way. "A lamb to the slaughter." I didn't know what that meant. "You be nice to that child, OK? Not going to be easy for her."

I said OK, but he didn't need to tell me. I had already decided for myself that I wanted to get to know her, if just to see what I could find out. A real Yankee! If she had come from the moon, it wouldn't have been more exotic. It was around that time that I had begun to feel a tug toward other worlds outside of Tifton. I'd seen what Hollywood presented in the movies, and I had read in books about other lives and other places. I was hungry for more.

I spotted Linda the next morning at school when she and her mother got out of their car in the parking lot and walked toward the building. It had to be her because she was the only kid at school that I didn't know. She had the longest ponytail I'd ever seen, dark brown and wavy, hanging down past her waist. It swished side to side when she walked. I wondered if all Yankee girls had long ponytails.

After lunch that day, I saw her at recess. She stood by herself right close by the big loblolly pine tree in the middle of the yard, clutching a rolled-up sweater tight against her chest, like a drowning person hanging onto a life jacket. I went over to her. "Hi," I said. "You're the new girl." It was a silly thing to say but all I could think of.

She looked suspicious of me at first. Then she tried to smile. I could tell it was an effort. "My name is Linda. I just moved here last week," she said, like she truly wasn't aware that everybody already knew exactly how long she had been here, and what her name was. Her voice was not like ours but not as unpleasant as I had expected. She sounded a little like people in the movies. It made me self-conscious of how slow I talked.

"I'm Judy," I said. "I like your hair."

Linda smiled for real then. "I like yours too," she said.

"Are you a Methodist or a Baptist?" I asked. It didn't occur to me that she might be neither.

"Methodist," she answered.

"Me too," I said. "Where are you from?"

"Huron," she said. Then when I said I didn't know Huron, she added, "South Dakota."

"Oh," I said. "That's one of those rectangular-shaped states right up close to Canada. Right?"

She said it was.

Corky Jackson opened the doors to the school building then, like he did every day after recess, and stood by while we filed in. When Linda and I walked through, he stuck out his hand to shake hers and said, "Welcome." I hoped other people would be nice to her too.

Not everybody was. Since I wasn't in her homeroom class, I didn't see all that went on, but I heard a lot of people calling her "Yankee girl" at recess and after school. They said it laughing, like it was a joke, but we all knew it wasn't. Linda didn't laugh. In fact, it looked to me like she did all she could to keep from crying when someone yelled "Yankee girl!"

She didn't cry, though. What she did to hit back was to be good. Linda was probably the best twelve-year-old girl ever to live in the history of the world. If a teacher asked for a volunteer to help out, no matter what for, her hand went up. She was always kind, even to the poor kids who were not clean and smelled bad, offering to help them with their work or sharing her lunch. She smiled like sunshine, if you even glanced at her, and made you feel like you were special. If she ever had a bad day or got angry, she kept it somewhere so deep nobody knew.

One day, she came to school with new information she had gotten from her mother, that she had been born in Missouri, somewhere fifty miles south of the Mason-Dixon Line. "My mother said that means I'm not a Yankee!" she said. Gradually, with her new credentials, as well as with her being extremely likable, most people began to accept her. On top of everything else, she sang so sweetly, just to hear her made you stop and catch your breath. Mrs. Andrews let her have some solo parts. She had made a place for herself. She had made a place, but she would always be "the Yankee."

You had to be born in Tifton to really fit in. The unwritten rule book for fitting in had a million dos and don'ts that people who were born here understood, and if you were not born here, you never did. On the surface, what most people saw about Linda that made her different were things like how her clothes were a little off. She didn't starch her blouses or skirts, so they were limp. She didn't have the same casual attitude about school that the rest of us had. She was a serious student. And she had to learn how to say "yes, ma'am," "no, ma'am," "no, sir," and "yes, sir" after she got a talking-to the first time she answered a teacher with just a "yes."

Then her mother topped it off with her own brand of being different. She wore dumpy housedresses instead of the capri pants and crisp blouses our mothers wore, and thick stockings rolled down around her ankles. Her hair was always disheveled. Our mothers made sure to tidy up their hair before they left the house and were constantly watching to see what other people said about them. Linda's mother didn't seem to care.

Another volume of the "rule book," as I thought of it, was about everything girls had to do to be "ladylike." The rules were endless. For example: "Never cross your legs at the knees, only at the ankles; then tuck them over to one side." "Never chew gum while you are walking. Always keep your lips closed together while chewing." "Keep your hands folded in your lap while sitting." "In church, never turn around and look behind you, unless you are at a wedding and the bride is coming in. Then you must turn and look at her."

Linda and I got close in church, at the Methodist Youth Fellowship. She and I were regulars, and we wound up hanging around the church. If there was a function going on, we were there. Sometimes we even went to the adult prayer meetings and Bible study. We were so familiar with the church, back rooms, Sunday School rooms, as well as the sanctuary and choir lofts, that we knew every inch of the place. We weren't especially devout like some people thought with all that hanging around the church. We were just comfortable there, like it was our private clubhouse. At the church, we didn't have to compete in the usual seventh-grade stuff, like parties and girl-boy doings. Church was easy.

The minister, Pastor Jimmy Cumming, had been a chaplain in the army and had recently retired from the service. His stiff bearing was a giveaway about that previous life. He had a wife and a couple of small boys not yet in school, who acted like little soldiers, being so disciplined that they sat unnaturally stiff through each service without squirming.

Mrs. Potter was the church secretary, young and pretty and married to one of the high school teachers. They had a couple of little girls about the same age as Pastor Jimmy's boys. Her office was next to his behind the sanctuary. Sometimes Mrs. Potter called Linda and me into her office to help her with mimeographing the bulletin or taking out her trash can or organizing shelves in the church library. It made us feel important.

Pastor Jimmy, who told us to just call him Jimmy, was often in Mrs. Potter's office. He always seemed more relaxed when he was there than anywhere else we saw him. Lots of afternoons all four of us sat around in Mrs. Potter's office, joking or working at some church project. Jimmy called us his "little church mice." It felt like we were a family, kind of a secret family in a secret world.

One afternoon a few weeks after Easter, Linda and I sat at the long table in the church library talking about God. I don't know if we were already bent that way, or if it was the influence of the location, but such subjects peppered our communication. "Do you believe all that about Jesus coming back from the dead?" she asked me.

"I'm not sure," I said. "Maybe he was just a prophet, or a teacher. How could he be dead and then not dead? Dead people are dead."

We chewed that heavy idea over back and forth until we exhausted all we had to say. As we were leaving, Jimmy called out to us from Mrs. Potter's office. We went in to say hello, and within a few minutes, Linda was talking about if Jesus came back from the dead or not. She asked Jimmy point blank, "Do you believe all that?"

Jimmy said, "I do. But I think the main thing Jesus and God want is for us to be joyful, and to help other people be joyful too. He mainly wants us to love one another." Then he gave Mrs. Potter a quick smile. Mrs. Potter's face turned red, and she got busy making notes in a tablet on her desk.

I recognized the two-second interaction between them, the little smile and Mrs. Potter looking embarrassed about it, as a grown-up thing that I didn't yet understand, and filed it away to ponder later. Whatever it was

113

between Jimmy and Mrs. Potter, it excluded Linda and me, but I didn't think it was all that important.

The next Sunday, Billy Jackson's daddy, a dentist, not a preacher, led the church service. He read from the Bible and had us sing a few hymns and the ushers take up collection, but Jimmy was nowhere to be seen. "The Reverend Cumming will be back next week, we think," Mr. Jackson stammered, like he wasn't sure he would. "He got, uh, called away suddenly. If Rev. Cumming can't be here, we'll have a substitute minister. Let's all remember to pray for our pastor." Linda and I thought it was odd but figured Jimmy would tell us about it when he came back.

My mother was in shorts sitting on the sofa with her feet propped on the coffee table and talking on the phone when I came home from school on Monday. Her voice had the outraged tone I'd heard before when she was shocked about something, like when our neighbor got fired from the Piggly Wiggly for no reason. "They took the discretionary fund with them!"

"What's a discretionary fund?" I asked when she put the instrument back in its cradle.

"Money the minister can use however he wants," she said. She looked at me in a way that made me uncomfortable, like she was trying to read my mind, like she thought I was hiding something. "What do you know about all this? You and Linda are around the church so much, you must have known."

"Known what?" I asked.

"You know they ran off together and took the discretionary fund with them, don't you?" she said.

"Who ran off?"

"Pastor Cumming and Sally Potter," she said. She gave me that look again, like I was guilty of something.

I couldn't understand what she was saying, like she was speaking another language. It didn't make sense. "Jimmy and Mrs. Potter? Why would they do that? Where did they go?" I asked. I felt shaky and sick to my stomach, like my whole world had turned upside down.

"I'm going over to Linda's," I said. I knew that Mrs. Brown and Linda, the Yankees who did not have the rule book, were the people I needed to be around right then.

Mrs. Brown came to the door. She had the same worried and disheveled look that she usually did, with her brows knitted together and her graying curls piled up in pins on top of her head, her housedress lapped across her belly and tied to keep it closed. "Come in, come in!" she said. She shook her head and put her arms around me. "Linda's in the kitchen. Let me get you a glass of lemonade."

Linda and I couldn't look at each other. We just sat at the table holding on to our icy glasses and stared out at her backyard. It was like we had done something wrong, like if we had been better friends to Jimmy and Mrs. Potter, they wouldn't have run off, or maybe if they were going to run off, they'd have told us, or even asked us to go with them. At the very least, it was clear that we didn't mean the same thing to Pastor Jimmy and Mrs. Potter that they meant to us. Nothing was what we had thought it was.

We didn't talk about it then. It was too confusing, but still, it was safe to just be there at Linda's house. I don't know what I'd have done that day without Linda and her mother, the Yankees.

***

After a study of religion in college, Linda went to Germany to get a PhD in German. When I married the first time, she served as my maid of honor. Then, a few years later, I returned the favor by being her matron of honor when she married David, a serious and appealing young man. Both of them became college professors, and he eventually became president of a small state college in Tennessee. Linda and I continue to stay in touch with birthday and Christmas cards, which are adorned with hand-written messages so dense they completely cover every available blank space on the cards. I see her only rarely, aside from the reunions, but when I do, it's like only yesterday that we were poking around the back rooms of the Methodist church in Tifton, talking and wondering about Jesus and God and trying to figure it all out.

Mrs Matthews

FALL 1955

"Let's all open our books," Mrs. Matthews said. "Turn to the first chapter, which is on page 12. Now let's look at the heading to see what it's about." She sounded like she was talking to first graders.

It was not a very promising start to the new school year. We were thirteen years old, or almost thirteen. We were not babies, and we were not stupid.

"Now," she said, "take a fresh piece of notebook paper and write down the title of that first chapter at the top of the page." She looked out at the class with a broad smile that didn't match what her eyes were saying, a dead giveaway to how nervous she was.

Mrs. Matthews was the new teacher for eighth-grade science. She was short and wore a brown suit and had short brown hair wound into tight little curls. She was not only new to the school but also new to town. The only information we had about her was that she had moved to Tifton with her husband, who was a professor at the agricultural college, and that they had no children. She had gotten the teaching job at the junior high after Miss Kennedy, who had been running eighth-grade science for a hundred years, had finally retired and moved to Macon to live with her sister.

The way things worked in Tifton was that the same teachers taught the same subjects for the same grades and in the same classrooms, year after year after year, so that you knew ahead of time who you were going to get for what class and just where the room would be. You knew which teachers were strict, and which were lenient, and which would allow gum chewing (three of them in the whole school), and which ones could crack a joke, and which ones were half crazy (only two that I knew of), and which ones were interesting, and which ones would bore you out of your mind.

And they knew you way before you showed up planted in your seat in their classroom. They knew who your mother was and who your daddy was and who your brother and sister were, and your aunts and uncles, and if you had cats or dogs and what their names were. So to have a new teacher was already something to be noted. Eighth grade was the last year at junior high school. We thought of ourselves as the seniors of the junior high. We were the biggest and oldest kids. We knew our way around. Next year we'd be at the high school and be demoted back down to freshmen, but this year, we were at the top of the heap and feeling the importance of the position. That is the main thing I have to offer in my own defense regarding these happenings.

I got out the piece of notebook paper, like Mrs. Matthews had said, and wrote "Overview of the Sciences" at the top of the sheet. It annoyed me to be following directions that I thought were useless and didn't make any sense, but I did it anyway.

It was boiling hot, like the first day of school always was. September was summer. It was not fall. But that day on the fourth of September, it was hotter than ever.

I had spent quite a bit of time choosing my "first day of school" outfit, as I was advised to do by *Seventeen* magazine, since I had a goal of making this the year everything would work out right. I'd discover the secret to being popular, so that I'd be in the in-group rather than the group that skirted around the edges of the in-group. I'd have friends bunched three deep around me at recess and get invited to all the parties and maybe have a boyfriend. Wearing the right outfit on the first day of school seemed important to achieving that goal.

I had picked out a blue, long-sleeved blouse, and a matching print, full skirt with a black elastic cinch belt. Under the skirt, I wore four crinoline petticoats which made the skirt stand out like a ballerina's tutu. The petticoats were a requirement for being in style. I thought I looked pretty good, but I had not given any thought to the weather when I chose the outfit. The people at Seventeen magazine only showed fall outfits as correct for the first day of school, and that was what I was going by.

I had science the last period, at two fifteen, the time when the classrooms were the hottest, after they had had all day long to store up humidity and heat. I sat at the desk I had been assigned toward the back of the room. All the windows had been pushed open as far as possible in a futile hope of catching a breeze, but since the windows lined only one wall and there was no cross ventilation, it was hot air, not a cool breeze, that poured in through the windows, like a furnace burning outside on the schoolyard lawn and funneling heat into the building.

I could hardly breathe with the cinch belt squeezing my middle, and the air that I could take in was half liquid anyway. To sit in a desk in the full skirt and all those petticoats, you had to lift up the petticoats and position them around you, bunched up in the back so that your butt was just about right on the seat. The backs of my legs were glued with sweat to the chair, and my forearms, with the long sleeves rolled up, stuck to the desktop and made a swishing sound every time I peeled them off.

"Do you all know how to outline chapters?" Mrs. Matthews asked the class. She looked around the room at blank faces. Nobody responded. "Well, I will show you!" She proceeded to write on the blackboard to demonstrate how to create an outline. The class didn't make a sound, although we'd been taught outlining in English last year. I thought outlining was the dullest, most ridiculous type of wasted effort possible.

I decided the class was going to be a dud and spent the remainder of the hour reading the chapter while Mrs. Matthews droned on and occasionally flashed that forced smile. I almost felt sorry for her.

"Now," she said, "listen carefully, because this instruction is about your grade for the class. You must outline every chapter in the book, as we come to it, of course. You will need to get a separate binder for science and keep your outlines in the binder. I will take them up at the end of each week to check them. In addition, we'll be having pop quizzes and tests, which will also figure into your grade."

When the bell rang at the end of class, I waited until everyone else left the room before I approached Mrs. Matthews at her desk. She looked worried. I smiled at her, trying to make her feel better.

"I'm Judy Ireland," I said. There was another Judy in the class. There were a bunch of Judys then, all of us named after Judy Garland, the movie star who was famous around the time we were born. Mrs. Matthews had called the roll at the beginning of the class but hadn't looked up to see who was answering, so I wanted to show her who I was.

"Yes," she said. "How can I help you?"

"I just wanted to tell you something, since you are new and all that," I said.

"Yes?" she said.

"Well," I said, "I won't be needing to outline the chapters. I know it's probably helpful for some students, but I'll do fine with simply reading and studying the book."

She looked puzzled. "Outlining the chapters is a requirement for the class, Judy," she said. "You might even find it a useful exercise."

"I don't need to do it," I said again, in a soft voice, trying to be polite but still make my point. "You don't know us yet, so there's no way you could know, but...well..." I hesitated. "I'm a good student. I always make As, and I've never had to outline a book to understand the material." I looked down at my feet in an attempt to appear modest.

When I looked up, Mrs. Matthews was staring at me, like she didn't believe what I'd said. I thought maybe I had not been clear enough. "Actually, I have never made a grade lower than an A," I added. "It's not a big thing, it's just that I'm smart. Everybody knows I'm smart." As soon as I said it, I knew it didn't help the situation.

It was true. It wasn't a big thing. It was just a thing, the same way that Sally Ann was pretty, and Martha had a rich daddy, and Billy had a beautiful voice, and June could play the piano better than anybody, and the twins could dance, and so on. I was smart. To be clear, I was book-smart. Common sense was another matter, and I'd been told plenty of times that I didn't have much of it, but that didn't apply here.

I didn't know how Mrs. Matthews would react, but I thought there was some possibility that she would thank me for letting her know I was smart, since it could help her be a better teacher. I mean, asking me to outline chapters in the science book would be like saying the twins had to dance to "Dear Little Buttercup" like four-year-olds, or that June had to practice "Twinkle, Twinkle, Little Star," when she could play "Clair de Lune" and almost make your heart stop because it was so beautiful. There had been times, listening to her, when I'd have traded being smart for playing piano like that, but no one ever offered me the choice.

I had always just been smart, and nobody acted like it was that special, but they also didn't deny it. Sometimes teachers got annoyed with me for blurting out answers. And it certainly did not help my social standing with the other kids to be smart. None of them acted like they thought it was a great advantage, although they didn't mind asking me to give them answers or how to do problems.

Mrs. Matthews stood up at that point. Even in her high-heeled shoes, she was shorter than I was, and she had to look up to me. "That's very nice that you are smart, Judy Ireland," she said. "And it's nice that you have always made As, but if you want to make an A in this class, you will outline the chapters like everyone else. If you don't, the highest grade you can make is a C. Is there anything else?"

I told her, "No, ma'am," and left the room.

The school year progressed. By the third week, I had given up dressing according to Seventeen magazine and had returned to wearing sleeveless blouses, which made the heat more tolerable. I'd also given up the idea of having a boyfriend, ever in my life, when I realized there wasn't a boy I liked that way in the whole school and that I truly loved Bernard Smith, my uncle's friend, and he was already grown up and in college, so it was hopeless. As far as being popular was concerned, I decided I was popular enough, and that I didn't want to go to every single party anyway. It wasn't true but telling myself it was helped.

In those three weeks, I had also not outlined one chapter in the science book. I don't believe I even thought about doing it. At the end of each week, when Mrs. Matthews took up the binders from the other students, I just smiled at her and shook my head, like we had an understanding. I also smiled at her when she handed back the quizzes and mine had the 100s written in red across the pages. I figured she had to believe by now what I had tried to tell her that first day, with the evidence provided by the tests.

The textbook was fairly interesting, and in fact, Mrs. Matthews turned out to be a decent teacher, so I didn't mind going to the class. If there was a piddling thought in the back of my mind that she would stick to her guns about outlining, I dismissed it. How could she give me a C, or even a B, when I so clearly knew the material?

During the fifth week of class, Mrs. Matthews announced that we'd have a six-week test the following Friday and that anybody who wanted to improve their score for the first grading period could do a special project. She said we could write a paper on the material we'd been studying or make some artwork that would demonstrate our knowledge. This appealed to me, so I purchased a large piece of heavy paper and created a poster with a drawing of a tree.

We'd been focused on an overview of various branches of science, so I drew a tree, the trunk of which was labeled "The Scientific Method," and detailed in script what that was. Then there were branches of the tree labeled "Earth Sciences," "Physical Sciences," "Biology," "Social Sciences," "Astronomy." Each branch had smaller branches coming off of it labeled with the subdivisions of science. I painted it in so that it was bright and colorful, along with containing all that information. It was really something. When I turned it in, Mrs. Matthews carried on about it and immediately hung it on her wall. We had the six-week test, and once again, I got an A+. I missed one question.

We got our report cards for the first six-week period in homeroom, which for me was Mrs. Webb's class. I flipped mine open and glanced at the grades. When I saw the C for my science grade, I felt the blood drain out of my face and nearly fainted. It was like a flash of lightning right then, that with that C I had lost a significant part of who I was. I dropped the card on the floor like it was a poisoned apple and didn't look at it again until Carol, who was sitting behind me, said, "You dropped your card." I picked it up gingerly with my thumb and forefinger like I was picking up a tissue that someone had just sneezed on and shoved it between the pages of my science book.

Walking home with Carol, I showed her the C.

"What will your parents do?" she asked. When I told her they wouldn't do anything, she said, "Why does it matter so much, then?"

"It's just that I've never made anything but As before," I said.

"Oh," she said. "So you won't be 'the girl who only made As' anymore." We walked on a while. Then she said, "I guess you'll have to be somebody else."

As I told Carol, my parents had never paid much attention to my grades. My grades were not very interesting. When all you get is A, A, A, who notices after a while? They did look at the markings for deportment on my report cards where I had not always gotten the highest marks. There were often comments about my not holding up my hand when I was supposed to, or having a messy desk, or talking in class, that kind of thing. I don't know how I expected them to react to the C, but they said little about it. Daddy just pointed at it and said, "What happened here?" On the deportment side of the card, Mrs. Matthews had written that I had chosen not to complete the assignments, but that there was still time before the end of the year to make it up, and still have an A for the year, if I wanted to do it.

That afternoon after school, I went to the dime store and bought a binder. I sat down at home and outlined the next chapter in the science book. It was tedious, but she had won, and I gave her that. It did not even bother me to do it.

***

I didn't worry too much about always getting As after Mrs. Matthews class. Maybe I was tired of being the girl who always made As anyway, before she helped me get over it. Even though I outlined the chapters and got my A for the year in her class, the C for that first 6-weeks-period was down in indelible ink on my report card for all time. My record had been broken. I could never again say honestly that I had never made a grade lower than an A. I found there was freedom in stepping down from that self-imposed pedestal. I didn't see Mrs. Matthews any more after eighth grade. I don't know how her life progressed, but I hope she was happy and that she got the rewards she deserved for her teaching skills. If I knew where she was now, I'd write her a long overdue thank-you note.

Lowell

FALL 1956

Clatter from the hallway woke me. Lowell was out there setting up the ironing board, like he did every morning. I stuck my head out of my bedroom door to see him bare-chested, fiddling with the catch with one hand, the iron in the other, and his green- and brown-striped shirt slung over his shoulder.

"I just ironed that shirt," I told him on my way to the bathroom, but he already knew that. He barely bothered to glance at me, like I was too much nothing to waste even that much energy on. Ironing was my job. Mother paid me $2.50 a week to do it, and it took a couple of hours every Saturday morning. And I was good at it. She had taught me how. She and Daddy were satisfied with my work. But Lowell was another matter. Nothing was good enough for him. Even when Mother ironed a shirt for him, it wasn't good enough. He had to go back and do it over.

And the shirts weren't the only thing. He polished his shoes every night, except the ones he called "dirty bucks," the tan buckskin loafers that were popular. Those he scuffed with a wire brush until they looked just like they did when they were new. And his hair. He used Butch Wax on his crew cut to make it stand up in front exactly like the Kingston Trio guys. When Lowell left the house, he was perfect.

"You're not dressed," he said. "We're leaving in ten minutes. You better be ready. I can't be late." He said all this to me while he passed the iron over the already pressed shirt.

I went back in my room and grabbed a blouse and skirt and put them on. "They don't match," he said when he saw me.

"Yes, they do," I said, but it made me wonder if they really did, and if people would be laughing at me behind my back because my clothes didn't go together. He shrugged his shoulders and returned to his ironing.

When we got in the car, Lowell in the front with Mother and me in the back by myself, he turned around and glanced at me again. "You're wearing lipstick?" he asked, like the very idea disgusted him. I'd just gotten the tube of pink lipstick, my first one, and already felt stupid about it without him saying anything. "You have it on wrong," he added. "It's too much. It ought to be just a little, and it's all smeary."

"Leave her alone," Mother said. She was driving to the high school, where Lowell was a senior, to drop him off first and then to the junior high for me. At the high school, Lowell bolted out of the car almost before she got the car stopped, slammed the door, and trotted toward a group of his friends. He hated being seen with us, especially with me.

Mother drove through the circle at the front of the junior high and let me out. My class shouldn't have even been there. We should have been at the high school. We were freshmen, at least officially. We were in the ninth grade. We had been at the junior high school campus since fourth grade, which made this our sixth year. It felt like we'd never get out of there, like the school superintendent would keep coming up with some excuse to make us stay forever, like we were little children like the kids running around who were half as big as us, playing chase and hide-and-go-seek during their recess, while we, at fourteen, just stood around in groups and chatted and tried to be cool like teenagers were supposed to be.

"They're having a B-team game tonight. Lowell's supposed to play," Mother said. "I'm going to go watch him. You want to go with me?"

"Maybe," I said. "I don't know." I should have said yes because I knew I'd go. But I was still stinging from Lowell's criticisms and wanted to act like I didn't care.

"He's just like that," Mother said. "Don't pay attention to him." She wanted me to go with her. Daddy was out of town, and she'd have to go by herself if I didn't go. He had started a new job, the third new job he'd had in two years, and was now a traveling salesman, selling service station equipment all over South Georgia. He usually came home on the weekends, but the B-team games were on Thursday nights, and he'd still be on the road tonight.

Not many people went to the B-team games. Mainly the parents and friends of the players showed up. And that night, at the end of October, it was chilly to be sitting outside on the bleachers. Mother and I huddled together for added warmth, which was nice because she was not a cuddly person and didn't think too much of hugs, but to sit close for warmth made sense to her and felt good to me.

We were only a few feet behind the bench where our players sat at the edge of the fifty-yard line, and Coach Turner paced back and forth in front of them wringing his hands. Lowell sat on the bench with the second string of the B-team. He hadn't been in the starting lineup as Mother had thought he'd be. He sat at the edge of his seat, leaning forward, jiggling his leg the way he did when he was nervous, ready to spring onto the field at the tiniest hint from Coach.

We were playing Adele's B-team, and it was not looking good for the Tifton Blue Devils. Halfway through the second quarter, we were down eighteen points. When Coach motioned for one of the boys on the field to come to him, Lowell leapt up and ran to him. "Let me go in, Coach. Let me get in there!" Coach put his hand on Lowell's shoulder and said something to him, which sent Lowell back to the bench. You could see his shoulders droop, even with all the padding in his uniform. I felt bad for him.

At halftime, the players trotted off the field, and all the spectators were left to find some other entertainment. The band didn't even come to play at halftime for the B-team games. The cheerleading squad, which usually included eight girls yelling and jumping and doing tricks at the regular games, got pared down to only three for the B-team games, and they didn't do much fancy stuff, just yelled a little and waved their pom-poms around.

Paula Hutchins, the head cheerleader, was there that night, along with a couple of other cheerleaders. She was one of the most popular girls in the high school. Everybody in town knew Paula. She had a headful of red curls and a beautiful smile that went all over her face and made anybody lucky enough to get one feel like it was the best thing to ever happen to them. She had never flashed that smile at me. I don't think she had ever even looked at me. But I'd been watching her all through the game, trying to memorize her moves, wondering if I could get my hair to do what hers did, wondering if I could learn how to smile like she did, or if that was something you had to be born with and couldn't learn how to do on your own.

When the players left the field, the other two cheerleaders ran down to where the PTA was selling Cokes, but Paula turned and looked right at Mother and me and marched over to us. I was struck dumb and just stared at her. It was as if an angel had dropped down from heaven to place jeweled diadems on our heads. Unlike me, Mother took it all in stride. Paula smiled at her, and she smiled back. "Hi, Mrs. Ireland!"

"Hello, Paula," Mother said. "Do you know Judy?"

Paula said, "Not really. But you're Lowell's sister. You enjoying the game?"

The cat still had my tongue, but I nodded that I was. Then Paula said she wished Coach would let Lowell play more. "Lowell's the hardest working one out there," she said. "Only reason Coach won't let him play is he's not filled out yet."

It was true. Lowell was tall but skinny. Paula went on, "That doesn't matter. He's really nice. We cheerleaders go to a lot of the practices and every one of the games, so I know. He's the nicest one on the team, including the varsity." She giggled, then added, "And I think he's the best-looking one too. Don't tell him I said that."

I worked hard at not letting my mouth drop open and at not saying anything to contradict her, but I guess it showed on my face. She laughed because she could see what I was thinking, and added, "Well, he's your brother!" Then she blessed Mother and me with another one of her smiles and popped off the bleacher and back onto the field.

"Paula comes in the store," Mother said, by way of explanation. She had to go to work a year ago to make some money so we could move out of Mama and Papa's house and had taken a job as a saleslady at the Diana Shop that carried women's clothing on Main Street. "When she does come in, she asks for me to wait on her. I think she likes Lowell." Mother beamed. People were always telling her they liked Lowell, that he was a nice boy, a good boy, a polite boy. I knew because I was often with her when they told her.

I don't think many people told her things like that about me. I was polite enough, but I didn't make up to people like Lowell did. In fact, I'd gotten into trouble at school a couple of times for telling a teacher she was wrong, or talking back, even when I didn't mean to. If a teacher said something that I knew was not right, I'd say so. Lowell never would have done that. He'd have gone along with whatever they were saying just to keep them happy with him.

"You need to learn to have tact," Mother said to me over and over.

I couldn't figure out what that meant. If something was right, it was right. If it was wrong, it was wrong. It didn't make sense to me to dance all around something that was a fact. Lowell got to play in the second half, and we won the game, which meant he was in a good mood driving home, telling us about a play he'd made and how he'd managed to tackle one of the Adele boys and bring him down. He was so excited about the game, it took him a few minutes to respond when I said that Paula Hutchins had come over to talk with us at halftime when he was in the locker room.

"Really?" he asked. "What'd she say?"

"Nothing," I said.

Mother grinned at him and said, "I think she likes you."

Lowell got all weird then, and said, "Well, don't say anything to her."

Mother said she thought that would be pretty awkward if Paula came in the shop and asked her to wait on her and she didn't say anything. Then Lowell said Mother could talk to her but that I couldn't. I said I wouldn't promise not to talk to Paula, and that if Paula Hutchins wanted to talk with me, I'd certainly talk with her, which set him off so that by the time we got home, he was angry again the way he usually was with me.

The very next week I was walking home from school, and Paula pulled up beside me in her daddy's station wagon and asked me if I wanted a ride. I was really surprised, and at first I told her no, but then she kept on asking, so I got in the back seat. There was another girl I didn't know in the front seat.

"This is Lowell's sister," Paula said.

The other girl said, "Oh! Lowell's sister! I'm Libby."

"You want to go to the Varsity and get a Coke?" Paula said.

The Varsity was the drive-in hamburger joint where the teenagers hung out. I'd never been there since my friends and I weren't old enough to drive, and I didn't know anybody with a car anyway, and even if I had, there was a certain level of sophistication we had not reached that would allow us to sit in a car under the overhang and wait for a carhop to come to the window and ask what we wanted. We'd have been impostors.

Of course I said yes, so there I was, a few minutes later, sitting in Paula Hutchins' back seat, sipping my Coke, trying to be cool, when I saw Lowell three cars away, laughing and looking all around, checking out who was in the other cars. It was funny to see him this way, instead of the way I usually did, glaring at me or working on his clothes. When he saw me, he stopped laughing, his face kind of dropped, and he just stared like he couldn't believe it. I smiled at him and gave a little wave. After that, he turned his whole body around so that I couldn't see his face anymore.

"So, who's Lowell taking to homecoming?" Libby asked.

I told her I didn't know and asked who she was going with. She told me a boy's name. Then she said Paula didn't have a date yet. I said maybe Lowell should take Paula. Both of them giggled at this, which I thought was odd since it was clear that was what they were trying to say all along.

"You could tell him," Libby said.

Paula swatted at Libby and said, "No! Don't do that!" But I could tell that was what she wanted me to do.

When we left the Varsity, Paula said she would drive me home and asked where we lived. I told her to drop me off at Linda's house because we were supposed to do our homework together, which was not true. I told her where Linda's house was and got out of the station wagon there. She and Libby waved real big and drove off.

After they left, I walked home. Linda's house was only three blocks away from the tiny house Mother had rented for us after we left Mama and Papa's. I had not thought about it before, but somehow, when Paula asked where we lived, I didn't want her and her friend driving up in front of the house and seeing it.

It just wasn't the kind of place where other people we knew lived. We'd moved there a year ago, but none of us had had any of our friends visit at the house. It was little. It only had two bedrooms, one for Mother and Daddy and one for me—because I was the girl, which Lowell said wasn't fair, and it wasn't, but that was how Mother had decided we would handle it. Lowell slept on a pull-out couch in the living room and had a chest of drawers in the hallway. We never talked about it, but Lowell and I, and probably our parents, knew we'd sleep there, eat there, bathe there, get dressed there, but we really had our lives at school, and at church, and at our friends' houses. Of course, sometimes Lowell's friends came to pick him up, and my friends' parents came to get me, but we were always waiting outside for them, ready to hop in the car. Mother had said it was all they could afford now, but maybe they could do better down the road, and we'd get a bigger house. We also knew that wasn't going to happen.

Lowell came in soon after I got to the house that afternoon. I was sitting at the kitchen table doing my homework, and he came and just stood in front of my chair and looked at me in a different way than usual, like he was waiting for me to say something. Finally I said, "What?"

He said, "What were you doing at the Varsity?"

I told him I thought Paula Hutchins must like me because she had asked me to go with her and had bought me a Coke and had given me some of her French fries.

I guess he couldn't think of anything else to say to that, so he shook his head and was walking away when I called out, "She wants you to ask her to homecoming."

"You think she'd go with me?" he said, like that would be some kind of miracle.

"I know she would," I said. "She only took me to the Varsity to get me to tell you she wants to go with you."

He still looked stunned, but he nodded his head and said, "OK." He walked down the hall toward his dresser. Then, after a few minutes, he came back and said, "Why don't you get your lipstick, and I'll show you how to put it on right. I've watched the girls do it. I can show you." I got the lipstick and brought it into the bathroom where he was and gave it to him. He pulled off the top and stroked it over my bottom lip, then said, "Rub your lips together back and forth," and showed me how to do it. "Now take a Kleenex and blot your lips." I did it the way he said, then checked in the bathroom mirror. "There," he said. "I guess you look all right."

***

After college and a stint in the army, Lowell went to law school at the University of Florida. He did very well: editor of the law review, valedictorian, star actor in the senior skit. After graduation, he took a clerkship with a firm in Gainesville, where the university is located, and has remained there to this day, eventually becoming a partner in the same firm. He is still in practice. He has fulfilled his early promise, pillar of the community, with a massive house that has a very fine bedroom he shares with his wife and golden Lab. There's not a pull-out sofa in the whole place. For every step I took away from the South, he took two in the opposite direction and became more and more wrapped in the ethos of the region, the very picture of a fine southern gentleman. If we stay away from discussions of politics, we can still enjoy each other's company.

Carol

FALL 1957

To write about Carol when we were growing up is to yank out my own liver and hold it out in front of me so I can look at it up close and write down what I see. She was that important to me, that vital to who I was. I stitched myself to her as tight as I could and spent all the time I was allowed at her house soaking up Aunt Ethelle's kindness and Carol's comfort with herself. And I was allowed to be at her house a lot. My parents sure didn't care that I was there. If Aunt Ethelle or Uncle Fred minded, I didn't know it.

Aunt Ethelle liked me, but then she liked everybody. Uncle Fred at least tolerated me. He was a shadowy man, like Papa Ireland, and didn't say anything one way or the other about my being there. Not in my presence, he didn't. Carol had two younger brothers and a younger sister, but they were, like her father, background noise to me. They were busy with their own doings when I was at their house. Maybe with four children in the family, the presence of one more didn't make much difference, and I could move in and out of the mix without causing too much of a stir. I moved in the mix more than out of it.

In addition to her being so self-confident while I generally stumbled around in the dark trying to figure out who I was, Carol differed from me in that she was short and chubby, and I was tall and stringy. I admired that. She was elegant. And she had the ability to be still while I never did.

Then, in the summer when she turned fifteen and I was still fourteen, Pinky Dennard pedaled by her house on his bicycle and yelled, "Hey, Petunia Pig!" at her. Carol had a crush on Pinky, who wasn't called that because of any communist leanings. His mother's name was Red, on account of her hair, and when Pinky was born with the same hair, they called him Pinky rather than Little Red or something like that.

Well, Pinky calling her fat hurt Carol's feelings. She never was one to go in a hole and brood about an upset, like I'd have done. She was a person of practical action and set about to lose the weight. She invented her own form of anorexia/bulimia. We didn't know those words. Maybe they didn't even exist then, but that's what she did. For that whole summer, she lived on Dexatrim, which she bought over the counter with babysitting money, and cigarettes she stole from her mother's purse, and black coffee. Whenever she did put a bite of food into her mouth, she just chewed it a few times then spit it into a paper napkin in her hand. Like everything else she did, she accomplished this with such grace that unless you were staring right at her with an eagle eye, you didn't know she was doing it. This was the bulimia part. But instead of swallowing the food and then vomiting it out in the toilet like normal bulimics do, she saved the bother of sending the food on a useless trip through her stomach.

Pretty shortly, she was so skinny her ribs stuck out like the fish bones in a Tom and Jerry cartoon, and her cheeks shrunk from full and rounded to as hollow as an empty bucket. You'd have thought that the adults, like her parents, would have gotten concerned, but nobody did. If anyone asked what was going on with Carol, Aunt Ethelle just said she had decided to "drop a few pounds."

Carol's weight-loss program worked to the extent that in the fall when school started, Pinky asked her for a date. I was as excited as she was, because if Carol was going on a date, there was hope for me too. Neither of us had ever been on a date before, which made me wonder if there was something wrong with us, since we figured, on advice from Elvis and the Everly Brothers and Buddy Holly, that we should be in love by this point in our lives, and dating was apparently the necessary precursor to the love part. Carol going on a date meant we were on our way to meeting that rock-and-roll standard.

Carol acted as casual as she could when she told her mother she had a date with Pinky, like it was a done deal, but it didn't work. Aunt Ethelle said she'd only allow it if it was a double date, so I got included in the arrangement. Carol told Pinky he had to find a boy for me. And since Pinky was fifteen like us and didn't have a driver's license, he said he'd try to find someone who had that credential to participate. He said that before he knew about the double date requirement, he had planned to have his father drive them somewhere and pick them back up, but this was better all around.

Carol and I made plans. "I'll be at your house right after I finish my chores on Saturday," I said. When I'd told Mother about the date, she'd been fine with it as long as I did my Saturday chores before I left. The boys were going to pick us up at Carol's at seven thirty and return us there at ten thirty. I'd spend the night at her house. My father dropped me off at noon with my bundle of clothes.

"Do you know where we're going?" I asked Carol.

"No," she said. "He just asked if I wanted to go on a date with him and I said yes. Is it OK to ask where you're going? It seems like it may be rude to ask, like maybe you care more about that than just about going with him."

"I don't know," I said. "Sally Ann said she goes to the drive-in with Bobby since he got his driver's license."

"Some people go to the youth center," Carol said.

"I heard Tommy Waldrop talk about going out to Willacoochee and looking for the swamp gas," I said.

"That's a weird thing to do," Carol said. "Let's get ready."

A few hours later, Aunt Ethelle leaned against the doorframe of Carol's room and watched while I unwrapped Carol's hair from large, pink plastic rollers. Light brown curls sprung back against her head. "You look like Shirley Temple," Aunt Ethelle chuckled. "Don't comb it out! Just let it stay like that. I'll get you a blue bow to tie in it." I knew she was being playful to get us to relax. We were nervous. She could read us like a book.

"Mom!" Carol pleaded.

"Tell me again where you're going," Aunt Ethelle said. "Did you say the movies? What's playing?"

Carol hedged. "Yes, I think so. I don't know. Are you supposed to ask the boy where you're going?"

Aunt Ethelle stood up and dropped the playfulness. "You don't know where you're going? You told me you were going to the show, Carol."

"We are," Carol said with a straight face. "I just don't know what's playing. That's all."

"And yes," Aunt Ethelle said. "When a boy asks you for a date, he's supposed to tell you what he's asking you to do. Otherwise you don't go with him. You hear?"

We said, "Yes, ma'am," and Aunt Ethelle left us to work on ourselves for another couple of hours.

133

The boy Pinky found for me was a year older than we were, gangly and in bad need of orthodontia. His name was William, and he lived out in the county and had gone to school out there until this year, which was why we'd never met him before.

The boys came to the door to get us right at seven thirty. They looked as scrubbed and pressed as we were and smelled of Old Spice shaving lotion, like our fathers, but I don't think they could have come up with one whisker between them. Carol flashed a smile at them which I recognized as straight out of Gone with the Wind, the part when Scarlett was flirting with the boys at the barbecue. She dipped her head and batted her eyelids, but I just looked at William and mumbled, "Pleased to meet you." He mumbled something back. After that, neither he nor I said more than a dozen words the rest of the evening. I was scared that anything I said would be wrong or silly. I don't know why he didn't say anything, but I guess he was scared too.

The "date" consisted of driving around in William's car, a green '56 Ford that was polished to a bright shine like a fresh-picked watermelon. We cruised up and down Main Street with him honking his horn at kids he recognized and finally pulled into the Varsity, where the boys ordered us Cokes and French fries. After we finished the snack, they took us back to Carol's and walked us to the door. Carol and I had had a long discussion earlier in the day about what to do if they tried to kiss us, but neither of them did. We got home at nine thirty, an hour before our curfew.

We knew we were supposed to tell them we had had a good time, so we did, but I was lying. I thought the whole thing was an enormous bore. I'd have preferred we stayed home and played Monopoly. Carol confided that Pinky had held her hand in the back seat and that she liked it. Still, she admitted she had hoped the evening would have been more fun.

Later that night, I complained to Carol that perhaps the problem was with Tifton, rather than with the boys or with us. "Not one thing ever happens here," I said. Carol sat on the floor in her bedroom with strips of twisted toilet paper woven in and out between her toes. She was painting her toenails peppermint pink. I sat cross-legged on her bed and flipped through Seventeen magazine. We were wearing matching, cotton, baby-doll pajamas printed with blue kittens chasing balls of yarn. The bed was our great-grandfather's—dark walnut, fruit and leaves carved into the headboard, which was so tall it almost reached the ceiling. Carol's feet were little and her toes curled up like they were made for elves' slippers. My feet were not cute, and I was not interested in painting my toenails. It was two o'clock in the morning.

I continued my complaint. "Tifton is just a boring place. It's a tiny little town where we know everybody and their dogs and cats, and we know everything that has ever happened here, which is nothing!"

"So what?" Carol said. She had finished one set of toenails and was onto the next.

"I just thought the date would be more fun," I said. "Why are we here in this silly town anyway?"

"We're here because we belong here," Carol said. "We were born here, and our parents were born here, and our grandparents, except my daddy's daddy. He was born in Lafayette."

"We could go to Atlanta," I offered, in an attempt to whip up some interest in her. "Heck, we could even go to New York on the Greyhound bus."

"You are just being ridiculous now, Judy," she said, and screwed the top back on the nail polish bottle. "We don't have any money. We don't have jobs. We're fifteen. Our parents wouldn't even let us go to Sylvester by ourselves. Listen, didn't Tifton win the regional football championship this year? That's something."

"Yeah," I answered, "for B division teams. We were competing against four other little counties here in South Georgia, if you want to call that 'something happening.'"

Aunt Ethelle, in her nightgown and with rollers in her hair, opened the door to the bedroom. She was squinting from being awakened. My aunt was a saint and hardly ever got angry, but she was angry now. "You girls need to be quiet. You need to go to bed. Carol, your daddy has to work in the morning."

We answered, "Yes, ma'am, I'm sorry," and tried to put on a face to match. After she left, we tiptoed out of the bedroom, through the living room, and out the front door to the porch, where we fished a crumpled pack of Salem menthol cigarettes and matches out from under an upturned flower pot in the corner behind a bench. We sat in the rocking chairs and smoked and looked out at the still street and listened to the crickets.

It was so peaceful and sweet sitting there rocking and smoking in the quiet dark that I could feel myself getting sucked into the comfort of that world, but there was something needling me that resisted the impulse. So, like a dog with a bone, I said to Carol, "I'm going to show you how much nothing happens here. I'm going to go out there and lie flat down in the middle of 8th Avenue. If a car comes along, it will run over me and kill me."

Carol stared at me. "Why in the world would you do that?" she asked.

"Just to show you that nothing ever happens here," I said. "I am daring the world to make something happen." I expected her to protest, but she didn't.

"You do whatever you want to, then," she said. "I'll sit up on the porch and watch. I'll be here to call the ambulance when you need one."

I walked into the street in my bare feet. The gravel was rough and warm from the sun the previous day. I glanced back at Carol, who had lit another cigarette and was slowly rocking. It didn't look like she was going to come rescue me. I realized my pajamas were going to get dirty and wondered what I'd tell my mother about that.

"Do it if you're going to," Carol called, just loud enough for me to hear her.

Finally, I lay down on my back, stiff and straight. The asphalt smelled acrid. It was rough against my back and legs. I was scared. I told myself I could get hit and die any minute, but at least something would have happened. I heard a rumble coming up through the pavement. It sounded like a car, and I sat up and looked back. But then the rumbling faded, and I could tell the car was on a side street, so I lay back down. After a while, I felt more comfortable and spread out my legs and arms with the warmth of the asphalt seeping into my body. I closed my eyes and pondered the mysteries of my own death. I thought about how sad everyone would be, and how much Carol would miss me and be sorry that she didn't stop me from lying in the street.

When I opened my eyes, Carol was standing over me with her hands on her hips. "Judy, this is just stupid and silly," she said. "Get up and come on in the house. It's time for us to go to bed."

I did. She never said anything about it again. In addition to being wise, Carol was kind.

***

Carol stayed in Tifton after high school to go to the community college and study business. She met a pre-pharmacy student there and married him after a year, and they went off to Athens to the University of Georgia for him to complete his degree. They had a baby girl while he was still in school. The marriage didn't last long after he started working as a druggist, so she moved to Atlanta, where her parents had moved after Mama died. She completed a degree in criminal justice and worked for the board of education in Atlanta until she retired. She now lives with her daughter and son-in-law in North Carolina and has grandchildren and great-grandchildren who keep her busy and happy.

She and I talk on the phone every week. She is still Carol, only more so as she has gotten older. She still calls me on any lies I might try to tell myself, for which I am grateful. Unfortunately, not everyone in her life has always appreciated her gift for truth telling. It's their loss when they haven't.

Sheila

FALL 1958

Linda and I sat cross-legged on the floor on either side of the big, square coffee table in Sheila's tiny apartment. The table was made out of rough slabs of wood and four-by-fours, the next step up from the planks and concrete blocks used to construct her two overstuffed bookcases. A daybed sofa completed her collection of furniture, unless you wanted to count the half dozen cushions scattered around the floor for additional seating. For artwork, posters of Picasso prints hung thumbtacked to her walls. The apartment was nothing like our own homes, burdened as they were with brocade sofas and drapes, spindle-legged tables, and heavy, framed pictures of landscapes and family portraits. We thought the apartment was the coolest place ever.

In fact, everything about Sheila was cool. Only a few months out of divinity school at Emory University in Atlanta, she didn't look much older than us, but she had privileges of adulthood. She lived by herself, with no parents to lay out her life and monitor her freedom. We were sixteen years old, juniors in high school that year, but Sheila treated us like equals. It was heady stuff. She had come to Tifton to be the youth director at the Methodist church. The church had never had a youth director before, and since Linda and I were youths, and were already at the church just about every time they opened the doors anyway, Linda and I took special ownership of her. She had no peers, no friends in town, so Linda and I stepped up to fill the role, ill-equipped as we were for the job.

Sheila was about as tall as me but quite thin, with very short hair and no hips, like the models in *Seventeen* magazine. She generally wore an enigmatic expression, like she was thinking of something amusing, but she would keep that to herself rather than tell you what it was. Even in the short time we had known her, we had found her to be funny and interesting, and it seemed like she really liked us. We could not believe our luck.

"Here you go," Sheila said. She handed Linda and me heavy mugs of coffee. Coffee had never crossed our lips before. Coffee was for adults. "You want milk and sugar?"

Linda said yes and shot me a look that said to not give us away.

I said, "Yes, thank you," playing pretend.

"I brought home the leftover donuts from the vestry meeting last night. I'll warm them up. They're still good," Sheila said. "How's the music? Too loud? You know that's Charlie Bird, right? You like jazz?"

"It's fine," Linda and I said in unison. It was the first time we had ever heard jazz, and "Charlie Bird" was my grandmother's pet parakeet.

The table in front of us held an assortment of deep-sounding books with authors like Martin Buber, Thomas Merton, and Saint Thomas Aquinas, instead of the *Saturday Evening Post* and *Life* magazines that lay in neat stacks on the coffee tables at our houses. We had been transported to another world.

I dumped three or four spoonfuls of sugar and a dollop of milk into the steaming liquid in the mug and took a sip. I shivered at the bitter taste and wondered why my parents willingly drank this stuff every morning, but I downed every drop with a straight face and tried to act like this was what I did all the time. Linda apparently had the same intent. I watched her grimace and swallow.

It was a Friday afternoon, early October. The summer heat had finally eased up a bit. That particular day after school, we had stopped by the church for Linda to get some music she needed for a solo part with the choir on Sunday, when we ran into Sheila.

"Come by and see my apartment," she said. "We'll have a housewarming!"

The apartment was the bottom floor of a duplex we generally passed on our way walking home, so we said we'd be there, and here we were.

Sheila brought out the warm, day-old donuts on a yellow tray and set them on the table. "Dinner!" she pronounced as she stuffed one into her mouth.

"Is that really what you are going to eat for dinner?" Linda asked, incredulous.

"If I want to," Sheila said. She laughed. "Is that weird?"

We assured her that no, it was OK, but at the same time, both of us imagined the horror on our mothers' faces if we tried to get away with eating stale donuts for dinner. Whatever rules applied outside these doors, out there in Tifton, Georgia, did not apply here in Sheila-land. I felt my eyes open wider than they had been a half hour before. This was solid evidence that other worlds, other ways of being, did actually exist, and that they might be attainable. I was drunk with the concept. The music, the brain-altering properties of the caffeine, the posters and the books with their evidence of a different kind of thinking, opened possibilities that had only been a vague longing before.

Sheila and her apartment became a magnet for us. I loved just being there and listening to her talk about her ideas and explain why she thought the way she did. She took on such topics as universal salvation, the shifting nature of truth, and why most other religions were just as valid as Christianity. By contrast, at my house, we talked about what was going on with our friends and relatives, and about how hot it was this late in the fall, and whether or not somebody needed to go to the A&P to get milk for tomorrow's breakfast.

So it was that one day when Linda and I were again sitting on the floor at Sheila's, listening to "the Bird" and drinking coffee, that I picked up one of the books on the table, *The Family of Man,* an oversized volume of photographs of people from different cultures, accompanied by appropriate quotations. I was stunned by the beauty of the book, which seemed to capture the heart of what it is to be human. One quote, "There is only one man, and his name is all man; there is only one woman, and her name is all woman," washed over me like a sudden ocean wave of understanding that our outward differences, including racial ones, are insignificant. My skin tingled, and I was moved to tears.

I looked up from the book and said in amazed wonder, "We're the same," like I had just been given the gift of sight, because I had. "They are all our brothers."

Sheila grinned at me. Race had not been one of the subjects she had covered in our talks previously. "Yeah!" she said, and stood, holding up her mug like the Statue of Liberty's lamp. "We're all one! They are all our brothers." Then she leaned down to look at the open page of the book and pointed to a woman. "Except that one," she said. "She's our sister." We chuckled at her joke.

Before I had this awareness, if I thought about it enough to formulate a coherent opinion, I'd have had to say I thought black people were certainly people but somehow less competent than white people. That was what I had inherited from my culture, as well as from my family. My parents were kind toward black people but kind the way you'd be toward an underling. My mother was fond of saying that black people were fine "as long as they stay in their place," which had puzzled me for a long time, and I had challenged her about what that place was. She couldn't answer other than to repeat, "Their place!"

It had to have been clear in the fall of 1958 that relations between whites and blacks were changing, with the *Brown v. Board of Education* decision in the Supreme Court, and Rosa Parks refusing to give up her seat on the bus. But in South Georgia, I don't think we truly expected the change to reach us.

"Do you see, Linda?" I said. "We are just like Negroes. We only look different!"

Even though she was from the North, Linda and her family had prejudices of their own. "But can you trust them? I mean, like white people?" she said. She had not grown up with Rosa Parsons or Baby, or anyone like them.

"Depends on the person, don't you think, instead of the color of their skin," Sheila said. As we talked, Linda came to the same place as me, but through a process of critical thinking rather than the sudden burst of awareness that I had. It didn't matter how she came to it. It became a secret knowledge we shared, a secret weight we bore.

There was no possibility we could talk to our parents about it. To tell my parents would have been an affront to their entire way of being, and not a cute kind of affront, like mooning over Elvis. It would undercut the fabric of their lives. To tell friends, likewise, meant we had crossed over into some neverland that set us even further outside acceptable limits of behavior than our bookishness and churchiness already did.

On the other hand, to carry the weight of our knowledge was an imperative to take some action. And we were idealists. We had to do something.

Later that school year, Mrs. Holder, the eleventh-grade English teacher, decided we should take up the study of debate. After a period of instruction, she said we would have a debate in class. She suggested some possible topics, one of which was school integration, and mentioned the Supreme Court decision. She asked for volunteers, and Linda and I jumped at the opportunity.

"We will be pro-integration," I said, after a quick glance at Linda. There were no other takers for the pro position. It was a perfect opportunity to present our ideas under cover of performing a school assignment.

Two farm boys were chosen to represent the anti-integration side. I knew immediately that this was going to be a bloodbath. The boys were no scholars. I should confess that I struggled with the sin of arrogance back then.

Sheila supplied us with ample materials to prepare for the debate. We had justifiable arguments for our position, and counterarguments for any possible stance the boys might take. The day of the debate, we ruthlessly ripped apart every effort they made to support segregation. Their final argument was that if integration of the schools took place, the races would begin to mix. Soon there would be intermarriage and thus mixed-race children. A murmur of disapproval arose from the room.

"You want to have a bunch of polka-dotted pickaninnies running around?" Johnny Smith asked. Giggles erupted. Mrs. Holder told the class to be quiet.

I had been waiting for this, armed with pictures of corn. "Hybrid vigor!" I proclaimed. I showed a picture of two ears of corn of different varieties. They looked like your average, everyday ears of corn, nothing special, except that one was more a yellowish color, and the other one a paler tint. Then, with a flourish, I whipped out a picture of a third ear of corn. It was the most glorious ear of corn imaginable, big and beautiful, with fat, shiny kernels about to burst with juice. "This is the result of interbreeding," I said, feeling like the champion in a wrestling match. "The same thing happens when people of different races marry and have children, a vastly improved version of either of the parents!" Here, I again pulled out the pictures of the now puny-looking parent ears to emphasize my point.

The boys' reaction, as well as that of the rest of the class, was general astonishment. What they didn't spell out was their repugnance at the idea of a black man and a white woman being together. They didn't even try to respond other than exclamations of disgust.

"Calm down now!" Mrs. Holder said. "We are making too much noise. Remember, this is just a debate! We must be respectful of others' positions!" Then she thanked both debate teams and said we could sit down.

"Who won?" I asked her. Of course, it was clear that we did, but I wanted her to say it. She only thanked us again and said we should sit down. After the class and after everyone else had left the room, I hung back until I was the only student there and repeated, "But who won?"

She shuffled papers on her desk and, without meeting my eyes, answered, "Well, you know that you and Linda did. You had very good research. And you presented it well." That was what I wanted. I had a terrible drive to win back then.

What we really won was a reputation that got us called "n—— lovers" for a while. It was mostly the farm kids who did it, and they didn't yell it. You could only hear them saying it when we walked by. The town kids just looked at us funny in a way that made you wonder what they were thinking. Then people seemed to forget about it, probably because they didn't want to think about the reality that changes were on the way, regardless of how they felt about them.

When we told her about it, Sheila congratulated us on the debate and gave us big hugs. It felt great to know that she was proud of us.

Sheila was in Tifton for about a year after what she called "the great debate," before there was a commotion that got her sent away.

Carol's mother was a telephone operator in town. When you made a phone call back then, you picked up the phone and told the operator the number, and she placed the call. The operators could listen in on any conversation if they wanted to. They weren't supposed to, but they did. Most people were aware of this and kept their conversations limited to what they didn't mind other people hearing. Well, Carol told me that Aunt Ethelle happened to hear some conversations on a long-distance call between Sheila and another woman where they were talking "like girlfriend and boyfriend." Carol said it really upset her mother to the point that she told the minister about it.

"What does that mean?" I asked her. "Like girlfriend and boyfriend? What did she say? I don't get it. Why did it bother your mother?"

Carol didn't know any more than that, except she said Aunt Ethelle was worried about Linda and me spending so much time with Sheila and felt like she had to protect us. Protection from what, she didn't know.

By then we were seniors, and caught up in senior stuff, so Linda and I weren't over at Sheila's as much as we had been before. Besides, Aunt Ethelle's concern was so vague that it didn't seem to mean anything anyway, and I forgot about it. Then one Sunday evening, some weeks later after Methodist Youth Fellowship, Sheila said she wanted to talk to us and asked us to come by her apartment the next day after school. I thought maybe she had some project she wanted us to work on with her.

Before we even went inside the door, we realized something was going on when we saw a stack of concrete blocks outside by the front stoop and recognized them as parts of Sheila's bookcase arrangement. I wondered briefly if she had invested in regular bookcases. But when we stepped into the apartment, we saw boxes of her books and rolled-up posters scattered around the floor. The walls were bare. Sheila just grinned at us and said, "Big changes happening!"

"Oh," Linda said. "You're moving. You got another apartment?"

"But why?" I said. "I always loved this one!"

"Y'all sit down," Sheila said, and pushed three of the floor cushions up around the square coffee table with her foot. That was when I got the feeling that she was not going to ask us to take on the refreshment committee for the youth fellowship or something like that. We all sat down cross-legged. Sheila clasped her hands on the table and looked down at them, almost like she was praying.

After a long moment, while Linda and I held our breath and waited, she took a big sigh. Then she looked at us and smiled in a sad kind of way. "I need to let you two know that I'm going to be leaving," she said. "I wanted to tell you, so you won't be so surprised if you hear it from somebody else, like Rev. Mathis."

Linda and I stared at her. It didn't seem real. We had come to take it for granted that Sheila was a permanent part of our lives. "Why?" I asked.

She shook her head and closed her lips in a tight way that looked like she was working at not saying something she wanted to say but couldn't. When she did answer, she said, "Some stuff came up. I have to leave it there. I'm sorry, but I can't go into it."

"But why?" I asked again.

"You have to trust me on this," Sheila said. "I can't say any more than that."

Then she unclasped her hands and held them out on the table, palms up. She was still smiling at us with that little, sad smile. I had the weird thought that she looked like Jesus. I could feel how much she loved us even though she had never said so, and all of us knew how much we loved her. There was like a kind of electricity going around among the three of us. I didn't understand what was happening. I just tried to hold onto it and feel it, even as it slipped away.

I did not want to cry, but when I saw Linda start to tear up, I couldn't hold back. Then all of us were crying, not loud sobbing, just desperate tears, grieving the losses ahead of us.

Our tears broke the moment, and we all took some deep breaths and got ourselves back together. Linda asked, "Where are you going?"

"I don't know yet," Sheila said. "But I know I'll be OK. Don't worry about me. I'll be fine, and so will you. I'll miss you, and you'll miss me, but we will all be fine. You remember that!" Then she stood up and told us she had a lot of work to do, and that she'd see us one more time next Sunday when she would tell the rest of the young people, but we shouldn't tell anyone before then.

Linda and I did as Sheila said. We didn't tell anybody.

I walked by Sheila's old apartment not long after she left and saw a young couple going into it. For a few moments, I wanted to go up and tell them to tread lightly in that place, and that it was hallowed ground. Of course, I didn't do it. I couldn't put words to what had happened there myself. I only knew that I wasn't the same person I had been before I'd been blessed to spend that time in Sheila-land.

***

I lost track of Sheila for thirty years until Linda learned, and told me, that she had gone back to the seminary soon after she left Tifton. She had completed a PhD in divinity and had been ordained as a minister as soon as it was allowed by the Methodist Church for women to be ordained. Linda said she had worked for years on various college campuses and had had a long-term relationship with another woman. I imagine she must have shined a light for hundreds of young people in her life, the same way she did for Linda and me.

Patrick and Marshall

SUMMER 1959

"Y'all want to go see the light?" Patrick tossed the question over his shoulder at Carol and me. He and his friend Marshall were horsing around with a football in Carol's front yard. Marshall took the ball and backed up fifteen feet away from him in quick little jumping steps then stopped and turned the ball around to get it just so in his right hand with his forefinger on the tip, three fingers on the laces, and thumb wrapped around underneath it. When he seemed satisfied, he lifted the ball over his head to feign a couple of passes before he let it go to glide in a perfect arc and nestle down into Patrick's hands like a trained pigeon flying home to roost.

It was the middle of August and so hot you didn't want to move your body any more than you absolutely had to. I didn't see how the boys could keep up all that activity in the heat and not melt into a puddle, but it was nice to watch them, as long as we ourselves didn't have to budge. Carol and I sat on her front porch steps in cutoffs and our daddies' old T-shirts and wished Patrick would give the ball back to Marshall so he could throw it again. It was like a dance, the way he moved his arms and legs and hips, and twisted his body in that elegant spiral to make the pass.

"You play?" Carol asked. If she'd even heard Patrick's question, she ignored it. Marshall was from Atlanta. He was eighteen, a year older than the rest of us.

"A little," Marshall said. "Used to, anyway."

Patrick lived with his father two doors down from Carol. His mother was dead. She had always been dead so far as we knew. He and his father had moved to Tifton from Atlanta when we were still in junior high school. He was sort of Carol's boyfriend, although she thought Patrick really liked her mother more than he liked her, and that that was why he hung out at her house so much instead of just because he was

146

crazy about her. But then, everybody hung out at Carol's house, and it was true that it was, at least partly, because it felt good to be around Aunt Ethelle.

Patrick and Marshall had been friends in Atlanta back when Patrick and his father lived there, and they still visited back and forth for a few weeks every summer. I had met Marshall during those other summers but never thought too much about him before. This year he had let his dark hair grow long and wore it slicked back with some kind of hair stuff, like Elvis. So there was the hair, but that wasn't all of it. I noticed for the first time that he had deep-set, brown eyes and a lopsided grin, also like Elvis. And there was the fact that he had already graduated and was on his way to college in a couple of weeks, while the rest of us were just getting ready to go into our senior year in high school in the fall. I was smitten with him.

The Tifton boys were not that interesting. They all looked like somebody's brother, which was probably because we'd been with them since we were born and remembered when they threw spitballs at us or picked their noses, and it was not possible to think about them in any romantic way without wanting to turn your head and feel a little disgusted.

"He hurt his knee," Patrick said. "Won't be able to play in college." He held onto the ball, like he knew how seriously we wanted to watch Marshall take it and roll it around in his hands again, and he didn't like Marshall getting all that attention. He was jealous. You could see that, even if he didn't know it himself. "Well, what about going to see the light?"

"I don't think Mom would let me go," Carol said. She lifted her hair up in back and fanned at her sweaty neck with her other hand.

"What if Patrick asked her?" I said, not willing to give up so easily. "She trusts Patrick. I really want to go. I can tell my mother I'm going with Carol, and she won't care." I knew she wouldn't care. She didn't ask too much about what I did. Mostly I was doing church stuff, anyway, so I think she figured that whatever I told her was OK and that I was a nice girl who wouldn't get into trouble anyway. In fact, I wanted to get into trouble. I just didn't know how, and it wasn't easy to find trouble to get into, especially since I wasn't even sure what trouble would look like if I came face-to-face with it.

"What's the light?" Marshall asked.

"It's this spot off a dirt road in a swamp out from Willacoochee, where you can go park at night and wait and sometimes you see these strange lights that jump around. Some people think it's ghosts. Others say it's swamp gas, whatever that is. I went down there once with a couple of guys, but we didn't see anything," Patrick said. "You have to catch it at exactly the right time, in the right conditions, like the right heat and the right humidity, and maybe the right phase of the moon."

"I've heard people say they've seen it," Carol contributed. "But I've never been there myself."

"Me neither," I said. "But I want to. I've wanted to ever since I first heard about it." I wondered if I was being a little too pushy. But it was true. I did want to go see the light. Although mainly, right then, I wanted to go because if we went, Marshall would be going too.

"I never heard of driving out in the swamp to see a light," Marshall said, shaking his head. "But I'll go if that's what y'all want to do."

You could tell he thought it was a stupid idea. It was probably something kids in Atlanta would never do, because life was a lot more interesting up there, and they had plenty of other things to do. No matter what he thought now, I hoped that maybe he'd change his mind if we actually did get to see the light.

Just like I predicted, Aunt Ethelle gave Patrick her OK to take us on the adventure. She just made him promise he'd get us back by midnight and said since it was going to take an hour to get there and an hour to get back, we'd better leave early. She made pimento cheese and ham sandwiches for us, wrapped them in wax paper, and packed them in a shoebox, along with some homemade chocolate chip cookies and half a bag of potato chips. "Y'all stop and get yourselves Coca-Colas to go with your picnic," she said. "I don't know where this light is, but there's got to be a gas station or something where you can get what else you need." With Aunt Ethelle, it was like she always wanted us to have a good time and was willing to help us do it.

I had to go home and tell my mother I was going and change clothes. Before I left, Carol said why didn't we wear our matching outfits. We had white jeans alike and halter tops made out of red bandannas. I'd made the tops myself because my grandmother Colley had taught me to sew. We hardly ever wore those outfits because we were afraid people would laugh at us, but Carol said she thought it would be fun that afternoon because we weren't going to see anybody but the boys anyway, and they might get a kick out of it.

When I got back to Carol's, and they saw me wearing the same thing she had on, Patrick laughed and asked if we had started singing in a girl group, and Aunt Ethelle said she hoped not because none of the women in the Ireland family could carry a tune in a bucket, and that we were sadly disillusioned if we thought we could. She was laughing when she said it, and you might think it would have hurt my feelings, but it didn't. It actually made me feel proud because that was the first time in my life anybody had called me a woman, instead of a girl. Marshall just looked at us and smiled his lopsided smile and shook his head again. I figured at that point that he thought we were all weird, and that if I'd ever had any chance of getting him to think of me in any way other than as a hick kid from a backwoods town, that chance was gone now.

Patrick had a 1955, two-tone, green and white Ford that his daddy had gotten for him for his last birthday, as soon as he got his driver's license. It was a nice car. Only a couple of our other friends had their own cars, and they were junkers that made you wonder when you stepped into them if you were going to get back from wherever you were going in them. Carol and I thought Mr. McNamara, Patrick's father, got stuff for Patrick because he felt sorry for him for not having a mother, and the car was just one more example of how he indulged him.

We stuck the shoebox in the back seat of the car about four o'clock and took off for Willacoochee, Carol and Patrick in the front, and Marshall and me in the back with the shoebox in between us. We rolled down all the windows and the wind blew in, keeping us cooler than we'd been all day. Patrick tuned the radio to WWTF, which blasted our favorite songs, Elvis and the Everly Brothers and Buddy Holly. I was ecstatic to be sitting with Marshall and kept smiling at him, and at the same time trying not to, so that he wouldn't be able to tell how much I liked him. When he smiled back, I couldn't imagine how the day could be any more perfect.

Twenty-five miles out of Tifton we saw a marker for Willacoochee, along with a sign that said 50 mph. Not one mile down the road, another speed limit sign said 25 mph. Then, almost before Patrick got the car slowed down, the speed limit was back up to fifty, and he sped up again.

About three minutes farther down the road, there was another sign, this time for twenty miles an hour. There weren't any houses or businesses on the road, just those signs popping up out of nowhere. Marshall had been studying the scene outside the window and commented, "Those signs are odd."

Patrick snorted and said, "Don't you worry, big guy. We do things different down here than in Atlanta," teasing Marshall, and showing Carol and me that even if we weren't Atlanta kids, we knew a thing or two that they might not know. He grinned at us to let us see that he was making a joke.

Marshall didn't laugh. Instead he said, "Speed trap. Be careful."

Right then, we heard a siren and turned around to see a police car behind us, flashing lights and everything.

"Oh Lord!" Patrick moaned. He drove the car over to the shoulder of the road, and the police car pulled in right behind us.

We stared back at the police car. The closest any of us had come to the current situation was in the movies. The drama was exaggerated when a couple of policemen swaggered up to the car, and one of them stuck his head in the window. He was big, with bulging muscles straining at his shirtsleeves, red-faced, a cigarette stuck in the corner of his mouth. Smoke from the cigarette curled inside the car, and all I could think about was that Patrick didn't let anybody smoke in his car, so this must be really upsetting to him.

"Boy," the policeman said, "give me your driver's license. You know how fast you were going?"

Patrick handed him his license and said, "Yes, sir. I was going about twenty-five right when I heard the sirens. I just saw that twenty-miles-per-hour sign, and I was slowing down fast as I could."

"Not fast enough, it looks like," the policeman said.

The second policeman came up to the car. He was skinny, wearing glasses, not as mean-looking as the other man, but he had a long flashlight, and even though it wasn't dark yet, he shined it into the front seat and then into our eyes in the back, peering at us like we'd done something wrong.

Marshall must have seen that I was scared. He put his hand on my knee and left it there, which made me feel better.

"Who are these girls?" the second policeman asked. "Why are they in that getup?"

"What getup?" Marshall asked. We'd all forgotten for a moment about our matching clothes. I nearly blurted out that Carol and I were just fooling around with the outfits, and how I had made the tops myself because I could sew, but before I could open my mouth, Marshall said, "They sing. We've got to get down to the Legion hall in Waycross for them to go onstage in about an hour."

I was shocked at hearing him tell such a bald-faced lie, and to a policeman at that, but I had enough sense to know the best thing I could do was keep my mouth closed.

"They your girlfriends?" the first policeman asked.

Marshall and Patrick answered at the same time, "Yes." Marshall pulled me over to him, put his arm around me and nearly crushed Aunt Ethelle's shoebox. My heart pounded away so hard, I was sure everybody could hear it. I didn't know if it was because I was scared, or because I was excited that Marshall had his arm around me, and, even if it was a lie, had said I was his girlfriend.

"OK," the first policeman said. "You're in a hurry, so maybe we should get on with it. I'm giving you a ticket for twenty-five dollars, for speeding. You have to come back down here next week to go to court to go before the judge. And you"—he pointed at Patrick—"being a minor, have to bring your parent or another responsible adult with you." He was still holding Patrick's driver's license. "Sometimes it can take more than one day to get through the court hearing, so be ready to stay here for forty-eight hours or more."

"My daddy said if I ever got a ticket, he'd take away my car." Patrick almost cried. "And he has a job. He can't take off that long to come down here." His voice was shaking.

The second policeman, the skinny one, said, "Well, you're up a creek, boy!"

The first policeman said, "If we have to, we can put all of you in the jail until court day next week, to make sure you'll be here."

Carol reached over the seat and took hold of my hand, and she and I started crying. Carol said, "No, no, no! We're going to get records!" As for me, I was too scared to say a word.

Then the first policeman turned to the second one and said, "They look like decent kids, don't you think, Joe? Maybe we could do them a favor, handle the court appearance ourselves, get the fine from them now and give it to the judge next week."

The second policeman, said, "I don't know," but then agreed. "OK. You kids are in luck. Give us the twenty-five dollars, and we'll take care of it. In fact, there's a special case here where if we do it this way, we don't even have to give you the ticket. Nobody, like your parents, has to know it even happened."

Patrick's voice was still shaking as he said, "But I don't have that much money, sir." Sweat poured off his face.

The first policeman said, "How about the rest of you? Y'all are in this together. I bet you can come up with twenty-five dollars between the four of you."

Carol and I grabbed our purses and started rummaging in them to see what kind of money we could find. I had a couple of dollars, and Carol had four and some change. Patrick pulled seven dollars out of his wallet. Marshall gathered all our money and counted it but didn't even look in his own wallet.

The two policemen leaned down to look in the car window. Marshall held onto the thirteen dollars but made no move to offer it to them. "Officers, sirs," he said. "We don't have the money for the fine. We need what we've got here to go to the girls' show and get back home."

The first policemen pulled a little notebook out of his pocket and began to write in it. "If that's how you want it, boy," he said. "Y'all get out of the car, and we'll get you over to the jail." Then Marshall got his driver's license out of his wallet and gave it to the first policeman and said, "Sir, I'm from Atlanta. My dad's a lawyer up there, sir, but he's tried some cases down here in South Georgia. Maybe you know him. His name's Bill Bolton. I promise you that we'll come back down here with Patrick next week, and he'll pay the fine in court. You can keep my license if you have to, to make sure we'll be back."

I knew for a fact that Marshall's father was a car salesman because Patrick's father had told us he bought Patrick's Ford from him in Atlanta.

"A lawyer?" the second policeman said.

"Never heard of any Bill Bolton," the first policeman said. "Have you, Joe?"

"He's from Atlanta, all right," the policeman holding Marshall's license said. Then the two of them walked off a few steps and had some words between them. It looked like they were arguing, with the skinny officer waving his hands and shaking his head, and the big one nodding and fiddling with his notebook. When they came back, he said, "This is your lucky day, kids! We decided we're going to let you off real easy this time." He gave Patrick and Marshall back their licenses and smiled big. "Only requirement is that we get to hear the girls sing one of their songs now, and we'll let you go."

"Fair enough!" Patrick said. He looked like he might faint from relief. I thought I was going to throw up. I gulped. "Oh God!"

Carol went white, like all the blood drained from her face. "I can't do it!" she cried.

Marshall stepped in again. "Officer, they will not be able to sing right now. You can see how scared they are, and we're late, and they're worried about their performance, and we've got to get them to Waycross as soon as possible. Please."

Carol was still breathing hard, but after a few minutes, she recovered and smiled up at the policemen. She batted her eyes at them and said between gulps, "You give us your names, and we'll let you know next time we have a show around here, and let you in for free, OK?"

The policemen did not give us their names. They said they'd look for posters with our pictures on them, and they'd get in touch with us.

The sensible thing to do might have been for us to hightail it back home and be grateful that we weren't in some rat-infested jail in the middle of nowhere, but that wasn't what we did. Patrick had something to prove. "I am, by golly, still going take you to see that light tonight!" he said, once we were back on the road. He was not going to let Marshall be the only hero in the car.

We got Cokes at a store a little piece down the highway and took them with us to have with our sandwiches when we got to the light-viewing spot, which was no more than a turnaround off the muddy dirt road. There were no other cars to be seen, no streetlights, no nothing except the raggedy bit of road, if you could even call it a road. As soon as Patrick turned off the car engine, and the radio stopped playing, we heard swamp sounds—frogs and crickets, and off a ways, what we thought was an alligator bellowing. There was also a lot of buzzing from the flock of mosquitoes that swarmed into the car windows, as you'd expect in a swamp at dusk. Patrick was prepared with an insect repellant coil that he lit to let the fumes run them off. I can't say that the aroma of the insect repellant helped our appetites, but it was effective at driving off the mosquitoes, so we ignored the smell and ate the sandwiches anyway. When the shoebox was empty, I put it on the floor and slid over to sit close to Marshall. He put his arm around me, and we started kissing without even building up to it, him telling me I was pretty, and how much he liked me and that kind of thing. Having recently been terrified broke down some of the rules. That applied to Carol and Patrick in the front seat as well, I observed.

Lost as we were in the wash of emotion and frustrated lust, it's a wonder we didn't miss the light. When Patrick yelled, "There it is!," I felt like I was somewhere deep underwater, and the muffled sound of his voice pulled me up into reality. We all stared gape-mouthed out the front window, and sure enough, ten feet in front of the car, an eerie spectacle of pale blue and yellow and pink light danced back and forth across the swampy gap between stands of cypress trees, then disappeared. Just when we thought the show was over, it came back again and did the same thing another time. It went on like that for a good ten minutes before vanishing for good. It was beautiful and mysterious, and unlike anything we'd seen before.

We were all stunned, even Marshall, who cleared his throat before presenting an explanation. "Swamp gas. I've heard about it. It's phosphorescent gases that come out of the bog from decomposing organic material."

But Carol proclaimed, with authority in her voice, "Well, I think it's ghosts, friendly ghosts, beautiful ghosts! And I don't want to hear about decomposing organic material!"

I suggested both could be true, that ghosts could choose to inhabit swamp gas if they wanted to. Nobody else jumped in to endorse my thought, but that was OK.

Marshall was due to go back to Atlanta the next day on the Greyhound bus. Patrick drove him to the station, and Carol and I went along. A summer storm had come up with hard pelting rain and thunder and lightning strikes in the distance. When Marshall got out of the car, Patrick and Carol said goodbye there and told me they'd wait for me while I went inside the building with him for a few minutes.

By the time we got to the door, we were dripping wet, but I didn't mind. It seemed romantic to have the rainwater pouring down my face like tears. We promised we'd write letters and would see each other again as soon as we could. Eventually, after a few more kisses and a long hug, I left. I was sure we were in love, because that was the only explanation I knew for all that kissing.

For the next few weeks, I mooned around and thought about Marshall almost constantly, doodling our intertwined initials and thinking about the wedding he and I would have and what our children would look like. A letter from him came within the week, crossing paths with the one I'd sent him. Our letters weren't memorable, just accounts of what was going on in our lives and vague notions about seeing each other again sometime. Our passion didn't make the leap onto paper, even the flower-scented stationary I purchased especially for my missives to him. We corresponded for perhaps a couple of months before enthusiasm waned on both our parts, and the letters stopped. I don't remember who wrote the last one. I do remember Aunt Ethelle telling me I'd fall in love a bunch more times in my life. I didn't believe her at first. But the passage of years has validated her prediction.

***

Patrick wasn't much of a student. He didn't want to go to college, so after we graduated from Tifton High that next spring, he went to Atlanta and worked with Marshall's father in his car dealership. He was apparently a talented salesman because he did well and eventually took over the business. He came to the ten- and twenty-year reunions but not any others. We saw him again when Aunt Ethelle died in Atlanta in 1994, and he came to her funeral with his wife, a pleasant woman our age. After the service, they came back to the house to visit, and when Carol mentioned going to see the light, we all had a good laugh.

Patrick filled us in on Marshall when we saw him at the funeral. He had gone into officer training school after getting his degree from the University of Tennessee and had a career in the navy. He had served during Vietnam but had lucked out, getting assignments to the Naval Postgraduate School in California and then to the Pentagon and never went overseas. That was all Patrick knew, but it was enough to make me smile.

Robbie Underwood

FALL 1959 - SPRING 1960

Uncle Wilton leapt to his feet. We were sitting on the ground level of the bleachers at the fifty-yard line. "I'll be danged! What's that boy's name again?"

"It's Robbie Underwood," I said. "That's the one Daddy was telling you about."

"Well, your daddy's right on the money! The boy sure knows his way around a football! I don't think I've ever seen anything like that on a high school field. Haven't seen much like it on a college field!"

Uncle Wilton was my daddy's baby brother and my favorite uncle, outdistancing whomever came in second by about a hundred miles. He and his wife lived in Jesup, but he came over to visit Mama and Papa every few weeks. He loved football. And it was a Friday night in October, and Uncle Wilton was in town. I didn't have a date, which wasn't that unusual, but my friends all did, or had other plans, which was unusual. Anyway, when Uncle Wilton asked if I wanted to go to the game, I was happy to go.

You'd think, being seventeen and a senior, I'd have been embarrassed to be seen with my uncle at the football game because it would make people wonder what was wrong with me that I didn't have a date. But in fact, I'd have gone anywhere with Uncle Wilton just for the pure pleasure of his company. He was more fun than anyone I have ever known before or since, so hilarious that lots of times I had to leave a room where he was holding forth because I was in pain from laughing and thought my sides would burst wide open if I stayed where I was

After we got to the field and found seats, it wasn't five minutes before Wilton had everyone around us laughing out loud, just hearing him talk about football, about Tifton, about politics, about driving the thirty-five miles from Jesup to Tifton. He could see the absurd in any situation and was happy to share his observations. I knew that's what he'd be doing at the game because that's what he did everywhere.

Then the game started, and Robbie Underwood started running the ball and dancing in and out around the Valdosta boys, and Uncle Wilton went dumb. He wasn't laughing now. He was astonished. I had not seen him at a loss for words before, but tonight, after seeing Robbie Underwood make three touchdowns, he could only shake his head and say over and over, "Dang!" and "Whoa!" and "Would you look at that!"

I didn't know much about football other than that the object was to get the ball from one end of the field to the other and then to kick the ball between the goalposts for extra points. In truth, I liked halftime, with the bands playing and the majorettes twirling their batons, better than the actual games. Ever since I'd given it any attention, Tifton had been somewhere in the lower levels of the division at the end of the season, and it didn't pay to get too invested in the Tifton Blue Devils. Some years we won two games, some years three. One year we won no games at all. This year, we had won all four games we had played so far. Everybody in town was worked up about it. The scores for the games were headline news in the Tifton Gazette every Saturday. Robbie Underwood got well-deserved credit for the change in our fortunes.

In the car on the way home Uncle Wilton asked, "Now, who are the boy's people? I used to know some Underwoods. Marvin Underwood, I think, lived on 18th Street."

I told him I didn't know who Robbie's people were, but that as I understood it, Robbie lived in the projects. Nobody talked about it, but we all kind of knew it. Only the poorest white people in the county lived in the projects, which consisted of four rows of concrete housing units, hunkered on the edge of the worst part of town.

"No!" Wilton exclaimed. "Is that a fact?"

I said it was.

Uncle Wilton was silent for a few minutes. Then he said, "Now, don't that beat all! You know as well as I do, Judy, that in this town, if you are just from the wrong side of the tracks, it don't matter how much education you get, or how much money you make, or how many souls you save, you are always and forever going to be the kid who grew up on the wrong side. You ain't never going to be nobody! And here we are, the town hero, the quarterback, making touchdown after touchdown, for God's sake, is a boy from the projects!"

Wilton put on that country-boy speech for effect. He knew about double negatives. He had a college degree, he was smart as a whip, he loved the English language, knew Shakespeare, could quote all kinds of poetry. It was just that when he wanted to make a point, he'd lapse into talking like that.

"Yeah," I said. "When we studied about India and the caste system, we all got it. It's not that different here."

It was just like Wilton to cut through right to the heart of a situation. But Wilton had his own bone to pick. He had moved away because, he said, "No matter how successful I become, I'll never get invited to join the country club in this county."

It wasn't that he particularly wanted to join the country club, but he might have wanted to be invited, since, young as he was, he was doing quite well and probably made more money than some of the people who were in the country club.

The next Monday at school, after talking about him with Uncle Wilton, I watched for Robbie Underwood out of curiosity. I wanted to get a close-up look at him. He had never been in any of my classes, and we ran in circles so different that, for all I knew, he could have spoken another language. About all I had noticed about him before was his big smile. He seemed to always be looking to catch everyone's eye, so he could flash that smile at them. Then he'd duck his head after he did it, like he was actually shy, and like the smile had been a major effort, and he was glad it was over.

I caught sight of him that Monday and noticed that he wasn't all that big, like some of the other players, and that his clothes were not quite right. His shirts were faded and plaid and out of style, and his jeans were too short. The other kids were saying, "Good game last week!" to him, so I said it too.

After that, whenever Uncle Wilton was around on a Friday night, if the Devils were playing in town, he went to see them. My daddy mentioned to me that Wilton was trying to get a scout from the University of Georgia Bulldogs to come to Tifton to watch Robbie play and see if they'd offer him a scholarship. Wilton had gone to Georgia on the G.I. Bill and had earned the first college degree in the family. After he graduated, he embraced the role of rabid supporter of the Bulldogs. Daddy said that it seemed really important to Wilton to have "that boy from the projects" playing on the Georgia field. Tifton High ended the year in football at the top of the division for the first time in anybody's memory.

Senior year was busy. I was dating a boy from Sylvester whom I'd met at a church conference. I only saw him every few weeks. He was nice, but the main thing for me was that it let me say I had a boyfriend, so I didn't feel bad about not having one. Carol and I were hanging out with a group of girls who got together on weekends for overnight parties, where we talked into the morning hours and planned and executed adventures like climbing fire towers, and going to the drive-in movies in our pajamas, and trying to learn how to smoke cigarettes. At church, Linda and I were busy leading a Sunday evening program for little kids at one of the missions in the county. Football wasn't much a part of my world.

Sometime after Christmas, we voted on superlatives for our class, to see who was the "sweetest," the "most likely to succeed," the "most talented," and so on. My brother, Lowell, had gotten the "neatest" in his class three years before, and I really hoped to get something, I didn't care what. I didn't want to care, but I did. I wound up not getting voted anything, although a friend who was in the group that counted the votes said I had almost as many votes for "prettiest" as Sally Ann Anderson, who won. Whether it was true or not, that assuaged my hurt feelings about being left out.

The big surprise about the superlatives was that Robbie Underwood was voted Mr. Tifton High School. You had to think about some kind of boy Cinderella when you heard the news. We had conducted a whisper campaign, "Vote for Robbie for Mr. THS. Tell everybody." But we didn't expect it to go anywhere. It felt subversive. In the past, it had always been one of the country club boys crowned with that most important title. When we found out that Robbie had won, everybody I knew was excited, like we had all accomplished something amazing. Maybe we thought that if Robbie could rise up out of the projects, the rest of us, who had much more minimal impediments, could achieve just about anything we wanted to as well.

Senior year continued to move along in a spirit of triumph. I got accepted to North Georgia College, where my brother Lowell was now a junior. It was as far away as I could go and still be in Georgia and have in-state tuition. My dream would have been to get farther away, some place like Oregon, but that wasn't realistic. Anyway, North Georgia had a reputation for excellence in pre-med, which I had fixed on as a worthwhile pursuit. Carol and the other girls in her group mostly decided to stay in Tifton and go to the community college and study business. Linda got accepted to Wesleyan College, a Methodist school in Macon, to study religion. My parents were moving to Miami as soon as I graduated from high school, so I planned to go on up to North Georgia right after graduation and attend summer school. I was finally getting out of Tifton.

Robbie won his scholarship. Uncle Wilton's football-scout buddy had come through. It was written up in the Gazette that Robbie would be playing for Georgia. The Florida fans and Georgia Tech fans were disappointed. I noticed that after the announcement came out, Robbie started hanging around with the country club boys. I'd see him get in their cars after school or just be standing around with them in their little groups like he was one of them now. It was interesting to me what was happening, and I wanted to watch and get the details so I could tell Uncle Wilton about it when I saw him.

Senior Week was a tradition in Tifton that held that seniors didn't have to attend the last week of school and didn't have to take final exams. Most of us drove around town during the day that week or went to the Varsity for Cokes and French fries. We didn't know what to do with ourselves. We made a point of driving by the school every day to see how it felt to watch the underclassmen still attending classes while we didn't have to. We'd expected to feel smug and superior to the sophomores and juniors plodding along with their heads bent down, worrying about finals, but instead, it drove in the point that the school was no longer ours, that the only slender thread still tying us to the last twelve years of our lives was graduation, and that, that thread would be severed in the next few days.

On Thursday of Senior Week, Carol called me at ten o'clock in the morning. "Are you awake?" she asked.

"Barely," I said. "You want to go cruise around?"

"Judy," she said. "Robbie's dead."

"What are you talking about?" I asked her. "That's not funny." Carol was like Uncle Wilton in that her humor sometimes came out in weird places.

160

"I didn't mean it to be funny. Listen to me," she said. "He was out with Freddie Wilson and Tommy Waldrop and Tommy Pratt last night, and they ran into that creek out on the Old Whiddon Mill Road. Robbie got killed, and the others are hurt but not bad."

My mouth went dry, and I couldn't say anything but "No, no, no."

"I'm coming over to get you," she said.

We got to the school to find most of our class grouped around the wide marble steps, crying or just standing silent. After a while, Mr. Coates, the principal, came out and moved among us not saying much, wiping his eyes, patting us on our backs. Nobody knew what to do. Finally Mrs. Burkhalter, the school secretary, came out and announced that we should look in the Gazette that afternoon, and there would be a notice about the funeral. We took that as a dismissal and gradually filtered back to cars or walked home.

The funeral was held at a Pentecostal church out near the projects. Robbie was laid out on a blue satin blanket in an open casket right below the choir stalls. It looked like everybody in town was there, and that all the florist shops for miles around had been emptied for the ceremony. People lined up out the door to file past Robbie and peer into his coffin to get one last look at him. When it came my turn, I got so caught up in staring at his face and how bizarre and fake he looked that Carol finally pushed me to move ahead. We didn't hear much of the sermon. I mostly watched his mother and little sister with a morbid fascination. The pain so clear on their faces was something you knew you could reach out and hold in your hand if you'd been close enough to them.

Graduation came the next day, on the heels of the funeral, like it was day two of the funeral rather than a separate event. It was like getting slapped by a second ocean wave after being knocked over by the first one, and you are still scrambling to get your feet back up under you when the second one comes to whack you down again.

During the last week of school, we'd practiced lining up in alphabetical order and marching from the back corner of the football field to the folding chairs lined up in rows at the fifty-yard line, so we knew what to do. Our chairs would have our names on cards taped to the backs. Upon arriving for the ceremony, dressed in our mortarboards and rented black gowns, we headed for that back corner while our parents climbed the bleachers and settled in to watch. I don't believe there was one person who didn't have a flashback of Robbie Underwood running down that same field clutching a football under his arm when they first glanced out at it.

We were a sad group as we found our places in line. The three boys who had been with Robbie in the car were missing. There was some speculation about why they had not come, but we closed ranks to fill in their places. Miss Hill came over and told the two people who had been positioned on either side of Robbie to leave a gap where he would have been. We started crying right then, a little bit. Then the band started up with "Pomp and Circumstance," and we began to march. We cried some more. When we got to the field, we saw Robbie's empty chair, his cap with the little "THS" charm dangling from the tassel, on his seat, and his gown draped over the back, and we cried again.

The speakers made brave efforts to move past Robbie's death to focus on the graduation, but their efforts were futile. Our hero was dead, and there was no getting around that reality. Special awards were announced and given out. I was given one for sociology and recognition for winning "star student" for having the highest SAT score, but all I could think about was that empty chair in the front row. When Mr. Coates called out "Robbie Underwood," for his diploma, his little sister marched up and accepted it. If a whole town can ache from sobbing, this town did.

After it was all over, and after we'd gotten hugs from our families, Carol and I and her group of girls, five of us, got in Carol's car and drove around, looking for someplace to go. It was late, and the only place open in town was the bus station. We sat in a booth with a metal table and cracked, red plastic upholstery on the benches, our fingers wrapped around icy green bottles of Coca-Cola. A pack of Kools lay on the table, and a couple of cigarettes burned, hardly touched, in ashtrays.

"You know," Carol said, "maybe it's a good thing he went out like that, at the most perfect time in his life. You never know. If he'd lived, he could have wound up slinking around town wearing his 1960 football jacket fifteen years from now, like Johnny Martin, hoping somebody would remember who he was and talking about that big play when he ran the ball seventy yards against Waycross." Johnny Martin was the high school hero in 1946, and he could still be seen some days, even in the summer, wearing that jacket and walking the downtown sidewalks, trying to get noticed. His mind was addled, and it was speculated that football had something to do with his condition.

"Yeah," Julia Paulk said. "But he might have done really well at the university and come home and shown everybody just what a boy from the projects could do."

"Even if he made a billion dollars and discovered a cure for polio," I said, "they'd never have invited him to join the country club." Uncle Wilton had read about Robbie in the local newspaper in Jesup and was as broken up about it as anybody. I figured if he had been sitting with us, he'd have said what I said.

***

Since then, at each of our high school reunions, the first item on the agenda is a somber reading of the names of those who have died since June 1960. The list, of course, gets longer and longer, as classmates are added in chronological order of their deaths. I wonder if the baby boomers do that, if they feel like they have to acknowledge the dead before they allow the living to have any fun, a glass of wine, maybe a listen to some old Elvis.

Anyway, Robbie Underwood is always the first name read. There is little more I can say about him, except that his life, brief as it was, continues to have meaning for me and probably for the others in our class as well. How could it not?

Epilogue

FALL 2015

On a May afternoon in 1960, in the last few weeks of my senior year, Daddy waited for me after school in the big boat of a car he had bought for his traveling salesman job. It was a two-toned, green and white Oldsmobile with fins that looked like you could hurt yourself on them if you bumped up against one. It was unusual for Daddy, or anybody, to come pick me up. I just always made my own way home, getting a ride with Carol, or walking, or finding somebody else going in the general direction of our house. So I knew something was up as soon as I saw him parked out in front of the school.

"Hey," I said, as I got in the front seat and stuffed my skirt and all the petticoats, four or five of them, into the car with me. "What's going on?"

"Just want to tell you some news," he said. "Thought I'd come get you and you could ride with me over to see Mama and Papa, and we could talk."

I have to admit I was mainly focused on myself at that time, with all the graduation activities coming up, and me going off to college right away, and I hadn't given much consideration to my parents' lives apart from my own. I thought everything with them was just like it always had been and always would be. I didn't expect them to make any big changes. It didn't occur to me that Daddy could have much to say that day that would be very important, especially by comparison to what was happening with me. But when I took a good look at him, I could see that he was not his usual lighthearted self, and I got a little worried about what he was going to tell me.

"What is it?" I asked. I was afraid that something had happened to Mama, with her bad heart.

"Your mother and I are leaving Tifton," he said.

I couldn't make sense of his words at first, like he was speaking in another language. But I understood his tone. It was the same tone he'd have used if he had been telling me Mama was bad off sick in the hospital. He was that somber.

He started up the car and backed out of the parking space. Some of my friends were walking by in clumps, laughing and calling out, "Hello, Mr. Ireland!" People liked Daddy. He nearly always had a joke or a way of teasing with them that made them feel good. But that day, he just gave a quick wave and drove on past them.

"You're leaving?" I repeated his words. "When? Where are you going? How long are you going to be gone?"

"We're going to Miami," he said. "We're moving down there. For good. We're not coming back."

I still half expected him to start laughing, to tell me it was a joke, and that he was just seeing if he could pull my leg. But when I looked at his face again, I knew it was true. He was serious, and I knew in that second that all of our lives were about to change in major ways.

"Why would you leave?" I asked.

"A man I met doing this traveling sales work offered me a good job down there," he said. "We're moving right after you graduate and get on your way to North Georgia."

I was stunned but stayed quiet and tried to just let what he was saying sink in and be real. He drove on toward Mama and Papa's house, going slower than he normally did, along the neat, tree-lined streets that we both knew by heart, both of us looking out the open windows with eyes wide, like we were seeing those streets and smelling the sweet springtime smell of confederate jasmine in the air, drinking it all in, for the first time. Knowing he'd be leaving, I think Daddy wanted to lay the picture down solid in his memory, so he could look back on it and enjoy it when he needed to. That was how it was for me.

He took a deep sigh and continued. "I've known for a long time that a body can't get ahead here in Tifton."

I thought about all the different jobs he had had, all the businesses he had bought, and how none of them had worked out the way he'd hoped and he'd had to sell them at a loss, and how he was always trying something new, and having big ideas about making a fortune, but never being able to make that happen. Maybe for the first time, I realized that he saw himself as a failure, although I never did. I might have been the only one who didn't.

"Wilton told me that same thing," I said.

"Well," he said, "he's right. There's lots of good people here, but you can find good people everywhere if you look. And here, there's some folks who want to keep you down, just because you've always been down, and they wouldn't know how to act if you got up." He thought about it for a moment, then added, "It's like I can breathe down there in Miami."

We didn't say anything else until we got to Mama and Papa's and Daddy parked the car in front of their house. We saw them every day or so anyway, so I hadn't thought about him having a special reason to go by there that particular day. But before he got out of the car, he said he was going in to tell them about him and Mother moving in a couple of months.

I prepared myself to have them be all upset about it. Mama got worried anytime anybody went anywhere anyway. She'd tell you to be careful if you were driving twenty miles to Sylvester and ask you to call her when you got home so she'd know you were safe. So I figured that for her to learn that Daddy and Mother were moving to Miami was going to cause a real problem, but it didn't. Mama just said that they would miss them, but if that was what he needed to do, then that was what he needed to do. Three of their five children had already moved out of Tifton, so I guess they were used to it. Or maybe they had the wisdom to know it would be better for him to leave, to get a new start somewhere else. Or maybe they were just tired. Whatever it was, they didn't make a fuss. In a way, I wished they had made at least a little bit of a fuss.

When we got back to our house, Mother had just come home from work and was still dressed in her high heels and nice clothes. She asked if Daddy had told me, and I said yes, and what did she think about it? Her response was like Mama and Papa's.

"It's OK," she said. "You know, we were in Miami during the war. He was stationed down there and he loved it, always wanted to go back. So now he's got this chance."

As soon as she finished saying that, she changed the subject. She went into telling me how I'd need to get the stuff in my room put into boxes for the movers before I left for college because they'd be leaving a few weeks after I did. She had not said how she, herself, felt about moving, so I let it go. I figured that if she didn't say she hated it, she was all right with it. And even if she wasn't, there was nothing I could do about it.

I went back to my room and lay down on the bed and considered the changes barreling down the road at all of us. It seemed like the announcement of the move was something that should have been accompanied by trumpets, by a choir of angels, or maybe by a funeral march. Instead, it was like a minor thing, like it was nothing, like a hundred years of our family being in this town could be wiped out by the offer of one good job in Miami. Even if it wasn't a perfect town, Tifton was our town. We owned it. It owned us.

The three of us sat at the table in the little dining room for dinner that night, surrounded by comforting smells of meat loaf and greens, which contrasted with the reality of the upheaval looming over us. For a while, the only topic of conversation was the meat loaf, which Mother had made with Mama's recipe, and she wondered if we thought it had too many onions in it.

When I couldn't be still any longer, I said to both of them, "Is it that easy to just walk away and leave everything about Tifton behind to go to a strange city where you don't know anybody, and nobody in your family has ever lived before?"

Daddy put down his fork and knife and reached over to take my hand. "Do you think this has been easy? I've been wanting to leave here for twenty years. It's taken me this long to put all the pieces together. And if you think any of us are leaving Tifton, you've got another thing coming. Wherever you go, wherever any of us go, Tifton is going to be tagging right along behind. You live in a place as long as we've been here, it's in your bones. It doesn't matter if you want it to be there, it is. It always will be." He let go of my hand and went back to his meat loaf.

I started to tear up, more out of relief than anything else, relief that it had been acknowledged that something big was happening. Leaving Tifton was not nothing. Mother had not said anything up to that point, but then she looked up from her plate and told me, "It's going to be OK. We're all going to be OK."

I didn't say anything else then, but later, trying to figure out what it meant for me, and how to move on inside myself, I could see that my expectation that my parents would stay forever, like my grandparents and great-grandparents had done, was important for me in part because it meant they'd be holding my place, so I could come back if things didn't work out for me in the outside world. With them gone, there would be no one, no nothing, to come back to. That was scary.

Mama and Papa would still be here, of course, for now. And Carol's family was here. But with my parents leaving, my connection to the town became temporary. My line in Tifton was soon to be severed. None of my children would ever hear the words, "You're a little Ireland, aren't you?" or "Isn't your mother one of the Colley girls? I think I went to school with her sister."

***

As my parents had planned, I left Tifton even before they did. Four days after graduation from Tifton High, I headed to Dahlonega, Georgia to pursue my higher education at North Georgia College. I loved everything about college—being on my own, my new friends, the classes, the professors. And I found I was exhilarated by living somewhere other than Tifton, being where everybody did not know who I was for two or three generations back and had already decided exactly which slot in the social order I was predestined to fit into.

After two years at North Georgia, I transferred to the University of Florida and finished up my degree there. Organic chemistry saved me from my initial vision of going to medical school, so I got a degree in biology. About ten years later, I got an advanced degree in psychology to do mental health counseling.

While I was in my senior year at the university, I met a good man who met all the right criteria. Right up at the top of the list was that he was a southerner. He was kind and innocent. We were both too young but didn't know it. We felt an imperative to marry and start producing children, which we did. We had three beautiful kids, and got consumed with parenting.

Twenty-five years later, after trouble in the marriage, and after all three children were in college, I fell in love with what my daddy would have called a "New York Yankee Jew." Those wouldn't have been pejorative words, just descriptive. I've been with this man now for thirty years, living in the San Francisco Bay Area.

Soon after I landed in California, I disposed of an apron that had a Confederate flag and the words "Rebel and Proud of It" emblazoned across the front. A friend had given it to me as a joke, but it didn't feel like a joke anymore. It felt like a label that no longer fit, even as a joke, even on an apron. A few years later, I took down from my dining room wall a prized antique picture of all the Confederate generals in a composite rendering. However, a small plaque that says "Thank you God for being born in the South and for cornbread and collard greens in my mouth" does hang in my kitchen. And if we're ever in a restaurant that serves grits, it makes me really happy.

My parents divorced within a few years of moving to Miami. They both remarried. You'd have had to be blind not to see that they were much happier the second time around. They are both gone now, of course.

Uncle Wilton died in 2012. He was interred in a small graveyard outside of Tifton, where his mother-in-law had been buried, and where he and my aunt decided to be put to join her when they left this earth. A few years later, Jerry and I drove to visit his grave on a side trip from our winter vacation in North Florida.

The graveyard is not easy to find. The tiny church to which it is attached is back off the main road that runs through a rural community that couldn't even be called a village. It's more like a wide spot in the road where there's a hardware/feed store and a gas station that does double duty as a convenience store.

We had been there for the funeral but couldn't remember how to get back to the graveyard and were following directions obtained from the hardware clerk. The dirt road to the church had been cut through an old pecan grove so that we didn't know for sure if we were on a public road or a farm road where we'd wind up at somebody's barn. Eventually, we saw a couple of houses on the right, and then the church appeared in a clearing on the left.

The church itself was obviously not in use, as grass and weeds grew up in the pathway to the front doors, although the graveyard seemed to be doing a brisk business, as some of the markers looked new. Only a small front yard had been left free of tombstones. A parking area on the far side of an alley behind the church provided space for a few vehicles, where several cars and a hearse were already parked when we got there.

We had only a vague idea of where to find Wilton's grave among all the others and were so intent on finding it that it was a while before I realized that a graveside service was being conducted at another site some way off. We were far enough away that I didn't think we were disturbing the mourners, but we still tried to move quietly while we continued our search.

When we found Wilton's marker, it was only thirty feet or so from the service, where a closed casket rested on straps above a gaping hole in the ground, beside a cloth-covered pile of dirt, with maybe twenty people lined up in folding chairs in front of it. They were dressed like anyone else you might see at a regular funeral, nearly all in black. The women had on high-heeled shoes, which, I imagined, had been a real nuisance while treading through that sandy dirt from the parking lot to the grave. Some of them wore black hats, and I could see a few with gloves on, very proper, very southern. The men were in suits and white shirts and ties. A priest in robes stood up at the head of the casket holding what I assumed was a prayer book. His words were muffled, so I figured if we couldn't hear them, they couldn't hear us, and so we continued with our mission.

Wilton's grave looked uncared for, which broke my heart. To see it covered in fallen branches and leaves from the pecan trees added to the pain of again being face-to-face with the actuality of his no longer being in the world. I started to tear up, and found a small tree limb to use as a rake, and began to clean it off as best I could. Jerry went back to the car and got an old towel to try to brush off the granite stone.

Just then, while we were completely engrossed in our work and talking softly about Wilton, and to Wilton, the Mamas and the Papas' "California Dreamin'" blasted out from the graveside service and startled us. I looked over to see the priest adjust a knob on a large boom box that rested on top of the dirt mound. The mourners sat in dignified silence with their heads bowed. Some of them dabbed at their eyes. Jerry and I just looked at each other in surprise. It wasn't the kind of music usually expected at a funeral service. Then Jerry asked, "How did they know we were coming?"

"California Dreamin'" was followed by some Elvis, then Bob Dylan prophesying about the "times a-changin'," and the crowd got up to file out in a solemn procession. Jerry and I finished what we could do with our limited supply of tools, and we said goodbye to Uncle Wilton. I didn't want to leave him there in that lonely place under that sandy dirt, but we had to. Life was waiting.

Acknowledgements

Thanks to all of those who read and encouraged my work early on—to Marian and Holly, who sat with me in our basement nibbling snacks, drinking wine and discussing our writing each month for years; to Phyllis and Adele, who read early drafts; to cousins Lainie and Martha, who read and approved; to Sari and Jonathan and Susan; to Deborah, who makes learning an adventure; to Tamim, who told me my stories "deserve to be read;" and, most importantly, to Jerry, my nearest and dearest.

I also thank April Gloaming for providing a platform for writing that takes the South out of the realm of the caricature and into the complexity of the wide world.

Judith Ireland lives in northern California with her husband, Jerry, and little Maltese, Charlie. Her story is in these pages.

Lightning Source UK Ltd.
Milton Keynes UK
UKHW041136130223
416928UK00003B/11